MURRAY ELLIOT BREEN

MURRAY ELLIOT BREEN

LIGHTHOUSES
OF
NEW ENGLAND

LIGHTHOUSES
OF
NEW ENGLAND

Donald W. Davidson

THE WELLFLEET PRESS

This one is for my mother and father,
who will always be our family's guiding lights
and for Bill Manchester,
who long ago helped me chart this course
and has ever since helped to keep my bearings straight.

Publishing Director: Frank Oppel
Composition: Meadowcomp Ltd.
Origination: Regent Publishing Services Limited
Printing: Leefung-Asco Printers Limited

ISBN: 1-55521-675-7

Manufactured in China

CONTENTS

THE HAZARD CALLED NEW ENGLAND

In the beginning America was New England, and New England was the coast. On moonless nights, her shore lay dark beneath the flicker of stars; on cloudy nights, her shore lay only that much darker still. And when the weather sullied nights with storms from any quadrant, this whole New England coastline lay then hidden as a hazard.

There was no loom from lighthouse lamps, no forlorn moan from foghorns. Not one dull clang from onshore bells tolled through the pitch of darkness. Along this stark, barren shore, not one such aid existed. On lands still bearing native names, like Monhegan and Annisquam, like Sankaty and Conimicut, then west and south to Noank, no New World needs had yet been found to justify such things. One day, however, New England's seaboard would reach from the St. Croix River clear down to the Hudson; along its western frontier, the inland waters of Lake Champlain would carry the Europeans deeper through the wilderness still. Until such time when names of land and needs of such were known, only fools or fearless men dared venture her dark waters.

By light of day, on the other hand, New England's coast seemed so much more attractive. First, as a subject of the Old World's curiosity; then, as an object of its wants. To these waters came the world's most celebrated voyagers with the collective intent of shedding upon New England's shore some light of their very own. Here sailed the cartographer Samuel de Champlain and the navigator Henry Hudson, as well as the adventuring Captain John Smith and the lesser-known Bartholomew Gosnold, all of whom followed the expeditions of those who remain known to most as little more than "Norsemen."

Whatever their goals and whatever their home ports, their route to this world was by water. Provided with little other choice, these mariners knew

No longer operated by the government, the restored tower of Fire Island Light still marks the way nightly through waters just south of New England.

Beyond Cape Neddick in Maine there is no other place in the world with a piece of geography that is known as a "nubble." Separated from the main-land by a gut of water, the land that sits beneath the Nubble Light is said by some to have been given its name from Captain John Smith; others say it came from Bartholomew Gosnold.

what the rest of the world most certainly understood: sailing the open Atlantic was one thing, but piloting near an unknown shore was altogether another. No one had maps yet of New England's land, and charts of these waters were sketchy at best. Instead, most shipmaster's would hold faith in those seasoned skills which had come from their practice of reading winds, judging currents,

and watching the sky for some sign. Aside from some guidance they found in the stars, their passage was surest by daylight; danger remained in the darkness.

Even the legendary Christopher Columbus, who has never been said to have sailed New England's waters, knew it better to heave-to at night than to approach any landfall past sundown. Though he was born to a family of weavers, perhaps he took heed of advice from his Uncle Antonio, who was keeper of the Genoa light, for on the deck of the *Santa Maria* in the early October evenings of 1492, Columbus bade his men to keep their keenest watch for any sign of land throughout the coming nights. After all, he had calculated that land was nigh, not due west of his Portugal where this New England would be one day claimed, but southwest of his starting point toward the Pacific shores.

Late on the night of October 11, 1492, Christopher Columbus was closer to these waters of New England than he was to those of the Far East, even closer than he was to home. And though he was about to discover some New World by surprise, his newfound coast would be as far away in kind from anything like that which ranged along New England.

Even before he made his landfall, one difference supposedly stood clear. Columbus claimed that he had spotted—four hours before any land—a light, "like a little wax candle rising and falling." Later, in the darkness of the early morning hours, a sandy cliff along the west horizon shone bright beneath re-

More exposed to the elements of the ferocious North Atlantic is the rock-bound Nova Scotian Lighthouse that marks the entrance to Halifax Harbour.

Race Rock Light etching, Fishers Island Sound.

Same as above, only a cutaway.

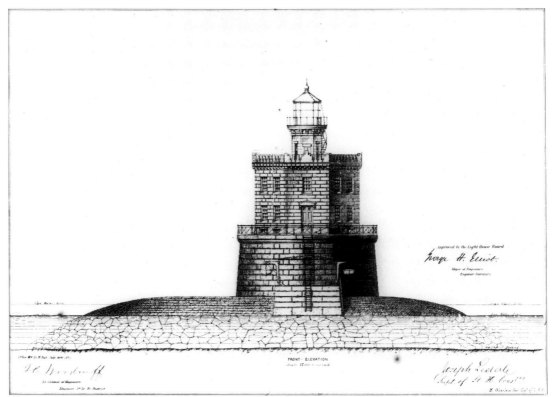

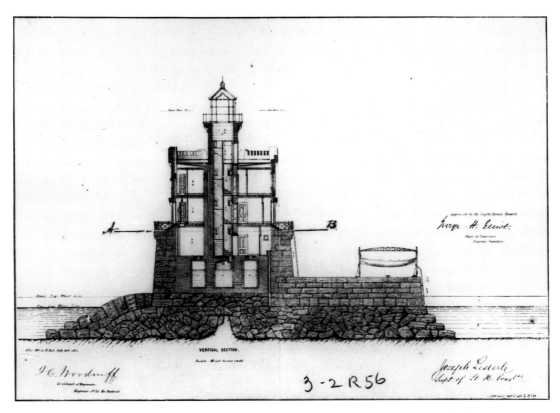

flections off of the moon, and the earlier cries of "Lumbre!" that had heralded the light, became huzzahs of "Tierra!" that harbingered their find. Though it was his long-sought landfall, as well as history's New World, San Salvador was not a coast as complex as New England's.

For one thing, the shoreline to the north had no such lights to guide a sailor into port or even warn him of an unseen danger; nor is it certain that Columbus ever saw one either. After all, America's first coastal light of record

Located off Fishers Island at the eastern entrance to Long Island Sound, Race Rock takes its name not only from the relentless flow of currents which endanger all vessels, but also from the rocks within the waters. These conditions accounted for the significant achievement of accomplishment when an offshore lighthouse was established here in 1878. To build this foundation, nearly 10,000 pounds of stones were fitted together. The masonry structure is almost identical to that of Stratford Shoal (Middleground) Light, also in Long Island Sound.

would not be lit until the glow that shone forth from Point Allerton, just south of Boston's harbor. Despite that supposition, any signal beacon from a New World beach in 1492 most likely would not shine with any intensity that could have been seen aboard the flagship *Santa Maria*, perhaps some 30 miles or more at sea. Yet, even if Columbus had been given guidance from ashore, he faced a coastline far less fearsome than that which others soon would see.

By the time Columbus had reported to Isabella, then set sail back toward Venezuela in 1498, John and Sebastian Cabot were voyaging from Newfoundland down to Virginia. Father and son both saw firsthand these northern waters rimmed with rock and haunted with its weather. A generation later, Giovanni da Verrazano would witness the same from the other direction once he rounded the sandy coastline that Gosnold would name Cape Cod; Champlain would call it Malle Barre. There, too, on the waters by Nantucket's shoals, was the horror of fog that could hug tightly to the boards of a deck.

Yet, even in sunshine there were dramatic extremes which sailors who followed would face in time. These differences were so much more than towering headlands and tidal marshes, so much more than thoroughfares and quiet coves, and so much more than unseen reefs and shoals that somehow shifted. Resolute and rugged, granite remained wherever it was found; sandbars, on the other hand, would wander with the waters and the winds. No sailor could ever be certain where such shallows might appear.

Regardless of whether the French had been the ones who named Vermont or Maine; the English, the ones who named New Hampshire or Rhode Island; or even the Native Americans, the ones who named Massachusetts or Connecticut, these rocky grounds were ridged long before. Through pristine valleys rivers had raced, channeling deep their courses toward the sea. The Kennebec and the Merrimack, the Presumscot and the Providence, and—longest of all—the Connecticut, whose name in native tongues meant "the long river." Some promised ships safe havens where their waters broadly bent, and many of them emptied into harbors even deeper.

Then not so far offshore huge rocks had fallen into place, roosting among the islands, some of which were nothing more than piles of rocks themselves. Legend recounts the story of how the Connecticut Indians had been embattled with the evil spirit Habbamoka for control of all the lands above Long Island Sound. Numbers were never enough when the mortals contested the force of any spirit; they needed, as well, whatever strengths could be mustered from all their beliefs in the world. Bolstered, then, with charms and chants, the warriors of Connecticut drove Habbamoka south to the coast near what would be named in years to come Throgs Neck.

There this evil spirit was almost trapped and overcome; however, an archipelago of rocks amazingly appeared, perhaps with an ebbing tide. Exposed, they not only served as his stepping stones toward the shorelands of Long Island, but also became his weapons of defense. From the safety of this land across the water, Habbamocka hurled at the Indians whatever boulders he could heft. Some fell to the ground along Connecticut, whiles others overshot their mark far northward past the coast of Maine.

In the Sound above Long Island's length, the pink-stoned Thimble Islands came to rest off of Connecticut's Stony Creek; Fishers Island and Race Rock fell into the Sound eight miles down from New London; and east and south of the Piscataqua's mouth, the grey-rocked Isle of Shoals was visible on some days be-

yond New Hampshire's beach. Further Down East, another 3,000 islands spread, one for almost every ragged mile of Maine's entire tidal length. Other New England islands would prove a lot more fragile, such as Newburyport's Plum Island, or the Vineyard's Chappaquiddick. Still, a few are more resistant, much like Vinal Haven and Block Island, Little Brewster and Aquidneck.

Named for Maine's native Cyrus H.K. Curtis, whose publishing empire included the Saturday Evening Post, Curtis Island Light welcomes the morning mists and the evening shadows at the foot of the Camden Hills.

Their names would prove to be as picturesque as the surf that pounds upon them. And though it was any number of men who took the time to name them, Nature was the only force diverse enough to lend them such intriguing forms. No mind of a man could have conjured up the splendors which enticed countless others to approach them at risk. And all of this landfall and water around it was fully the work of the water itself, first in the form of glaciers.

Lifetimes ago, ice sheet upon ice sheet plowed down from the distant north and covered this corner of granite and limestone and clay. At some parts, the thickness of ice measured nearly 2 miles deep. Harrowing earth, nudging its boulders, and furrowing channels wide and true, they stopped their advance as the climate grew warmer, then receded north covering tracks up with water. And aside from what else they had done to this world, they left in their wake New England.

This wake was the waters that sailors must travel; its legacy of land appeared like this: above its northeasternmost coast, the rising sun lit early the seaward

Under New Brunswick's jurisdiction, Cape Fourchu Light in Yarmouth, Nova Scotia towers above an island surrounded by the Atlantic Ocean, Yarmouth Harbour, and the famous Bay of Fundy.

peak of Cadillac. Towering hundreds of feet above the Gulf of Maine that surrounds Mount Desert Island, it reigns as the highest visible seamark along the entire Atlantic seaboard. At its feet are gathered the lesser heights: Baker Island, Bear Island, and Bass Harbor Head. Further out some 26 miles into the water, sits Mount Desert Rock, much as it always has. By night, of course, these headlands and islands and rocks by themselves serve no better as any aids to navigation than do the the south-stretching strands of Cape Cod. On the contrary, they long ranked among a countless list of hazards to be noted, and only those who had encountered them could have passed a warning on to others.

On Viking charts, in fact, a thousand years ago, the outer Cape was something they called "Straumey" a word that meant "an island with strong currents." Those Norsemen might have been the first to mark it so, and yet they surely would not be the last; the holders of the titles to the nearby shores off Chatham had agreed. They were a tribe of Wampanoag Indians who called themselves the Monomoyicks, from their Algonquian word "Munumuhkemoo" meaning "there is a mighty rush of water." These Monomoyicks, so it appears, had taken their own name from the waves and the currents and the tides around them, much as the land itself called Monomoy had been taken from underneath this constant flow of water. Such was the power of water to create an identity for the land, as well as for the

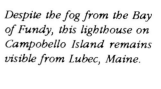

Despite the fog from the Bay of Fundy, this lighthouse on Campobello Island remains visible from Lubec, Maine.

people who lived upon it.

In addition, the water alongside New England has always since influenced its weather. Down from the northeast with freezing swirls, the Labrador Current eddies into the Gulf of Maine, first filling up, then funneling out the tides in the Bay of Fundy. Up from the southerly shores, warmer waters flow along Long Island, past Martha's Vineyard, then the island of Nantucket and beyond. These Gulf Stream waters drift from that quadrant of the compass where Columbus first landed. Just as the colder waters wash through narrow bays and inlets along Maine's erratic coast, these warmer waters race into the Narragansett, Mount Hope, and Buzzards Bays, as well as the sounds of Long Island, Martha's Vineyard, and Nantucket.

Before there would ever be any lights to mark the edges where water touched land at such places now called Goose Rock by Fox Island Thorofare, or Nobska Point on the southwestern corner of Cape Cod, there had only been the light of the sun to illuminate these passages and warm the days. Naturally, what the sun had always done to New England's waters it had also done to its land and the air above. With differing paces, it heated water, land, and air from dawn until the dusk; then, all at once it left them each to cool throughout the dark hours of the night.

The result along New England's coast has always meant a range of temperatures among the three, forever in a somewhat confusing state of flux. Always trying to even themselves out, they each must contend with the foibles of the others, so currents of water wash around the land, as well as beneath streams of air, while those same streams of air flow at the same time over the land and the water alike. In places such as Nantucket, or Chatham, or else Down East in Camden, that interplay of temperatures might create any sort of dirty weather, from fog in the summer to flurries of snow thereafter.

Such variations in temperatures have proved it difficult for even the most experienced of seamen to be able to fathom with any certainly the conditions from day to day. Perhaps if this corner of the coast that's called New England could be left to contend with just the weather it creates, then sailors might have fewer problems; however, New England's own little relationship among sun and shore and sea is often disrupted—for better or for worse—by whatever flows along the prevailing winds across the continent from the north and west and south, by whatever flows along the Gulf Stream up the eastern seaboard, and by whatever the shift of wind brings off the water.

In earlier days, these often appeared as tragedy: the howling nor'easter and the raging hurricane, both tending to appear with warning only to those who were aware of their earliest signs. For snow, it was often the look of the clouds; for wind, the uneasy feel of stillness, as well as the shape of the seas. And always for both, there was something to be sensed from the smell in the air. Those who would know such things would hearken to all their senses, and this is not hard to understand. Either a master knew that or he did not, and no lighthouse could offer much help.

All the while, the waves and currents that come from changes in the temperatures of New England's air and water have not been the only disturbing ways of the North Atlantic. The points and inlets that jut and break the length of its coast are also the work of lunar tides, those waves worldwide created by the tug of gravity. At the northern end of Monomoy's south island, for example, as well as at the northern island itself, the land is low and narrow from these tidal overflows. Further south, however, the coastline starts to flare and the beach begins to rise in windswept dunes.

Once the sands have exposed themselves above the surface of the ocean, the way of the winds picks up where the seas leave off. A single grain exposed on a sandbar only finds itself protected on the leeward side of a moonsnail's shell or the sprouting clump of beach grass, and soon a small but certain mound of sand can then begin to build. In time, this mound of sand drifts higher, only to become the first dune on a beach. This, in turn, will then protect the other sands from wind until the shoal becomes a barrier beach, such as this one off the coast of Chatham's mainland. There are others that stretch not so far away: inside Cape Cod Bay at Sandy Neck, just to the north of the Cape at Duxbury, to the south at Great Point on Nantucket, then west at Quonochontaug in Rhode Island, and even further west and south at Fire Island.

Just offshore from the Cape and Islands, the surrounding waters lend no greater comfort. To the south of Monomoy Point lies Pollock's Rip, the confluence of tidal currents from the ocean and the sound that even the scientists of the 19th century had recognized as being treacherous. "There is no other part of the world, perhaps," wrote the director of the United States Coast and

Where the waters of Nantucket Sound and Vineyard Sound tend to flow together, the noble Nobska Light stands watch from the Cape Cod mainland.

Geodetic Survey in 1869, "where tides of such very small rise and fall are accompanied by such strong currents running far out to sea."

So for decades, those who sailed to and from the waters of New England could only call upon their seafaring intelligence, their coastwise instinct, and their natural intuition to help them pilot vessels safely here from distant ports and then back home again. Basically, through their firsthand observations of New England, as well as their secondhand discussions with other seamen who might have experienced still different conditions in these parts, they came to understand in their own sort of way not only the water and the land of New England, but also the weather as well. In time, they found it worth their while to return. And then, at last, to stay.

Coming to grips with the realities which were New England demanded an understanding that must begin with the workings of the waters, and that is something that many a landlubber still sometimes fails to comprehend. Yet, it is those who are the most inclined to turn their faces toward the sun and their backs against the wind who still must learn to respect and to appreciate the hazards that once lingered at water's edge, at a time when water's edge was all that America was. Such is the heritage of America and New England, and one reason the lighthouse was needed.

A GLOW ON
THE HORIZON

When the *Angel Gabriel* appeared along New England's coast, chaos rained much as Judgment Day presaged. Storming ashore amidst the Hurricane of 1635 nearby the land that separated John and Muscongus Bays, she foundered off the coast of Maine when all of that was still a Massachusetts province. Enraged by the wind and foaming within its fury, these waters off the peninsula of Pemaquid had been plied, no doubt, in earlier years and on calmer days by the pinnace called *Virginia*, for it was not so far to the west of this shore that she had been built near Kennebec's mouth in 1607. There, too, in centuries ahead, more ships would be launched from this one spot than from anywhere else in America, and the *Virginia* is believed to have been the very first ever put together by Englishmen this side of the Atlantic. By the time the *Angel Gabriel* had finally settled down, however, the *Virginia* herself was already gone, wrecked off the Old World coast in 1628.

Gone as well from the Gulf of Maine by then was Dixey Bull, the very first pirate along this New World's seaboard. Plundered by settlers from France, whose European province had given this huge chunk of land its name, the Penobscot Bay trader set out to extract his revenge. Instead, Bull became a "buccaneer" who preyed upon other colonial traders and impressed their sailors into his band. After looting the trading stations at Pemaquid Harbor, Dixey Bull had hoped to make his way to the roguish Virginia colony before any armed authorities from Massachusetts Bay might capture him here in New England; however, he was foiled in his plan of flight, so by 1633 the pirate Bull had disappeared altogether, headed Down East to cast his lot among the Frenchmen after all.

The last sighting of the *Angel Gabriel*, then, was neither the most significant

Sitting on a ledge overlooking Herring Gut, the rubblestone tower of Maine's Marshall Point Light is joined by a walkway to the shore that holds the keeper's dwelling. Still the point of departure for the ferry and mailboat to Monhegan Island, Port Clyde was once the center of Gloucester's sardine industry.

Pemaquid Point Light rivals that of Portland Head and the Nubble for popularity with visitors who flock to the Maine coast to photograph these spectacular shoreline vistas.

of maritime events in the waters off Pemaquid, nor even the most colorful one. Instead, it was quite sadly all too typical of the colonial Maritimes. Given a good vessel on the open sea, a crew might live forever; however, in waters such as those of New England, closed and swift and often quite shallow, the best founded vessel with the ablest of seamen could never expect such good fortune. More often than not in these waters, peril was only a matter of time.

The very same storm which had overwhelmed the *Angel Gabriel* was described by Gov. William Bradford of Plimoth Plantation as "such a mighty storm of wind and raine as none living in these parts, either English or Indians, ever saw." Raging as far north as Cape Sable off the coast of Nova Scotia, the

hurricane scattered the crew and passengers of the *Angel Gabriel*, taking the lives of a fated five and tossing belongings from a hundred others, just as it had done with those of the *Watch and Wait* which was wrecked upon the granite rocks not too far north of Boston at Cape Ann. Four survived the ordeal of the *Watch and Wait*, while 15 others drowned. The family of passenger Anthony Thacher had the island of rocks later named for them, and it remains today known as Thachers Island. At the Isles of Shoals, not too many leagues from the coast of Kittery, Maine, the Rev. Richard Mather and his family had fared much better, surviving a storm-swept voyage aboard an English ship, the *James*. Out of Bristol, their ship had set sail alongside the *Angel Gabriel* nearly two months before. Clearly, then, some were more lucky than others, and that was the best that any crew might hope for. The same might be said of any passenger, which rated along with any member of the crew—below the value of any cargoes.

After all, much of the passage through the earliest routes consisted of seagoing vessels that carried new colonists here, then returned to Old World ports with fish in their holds, which were caught in New England's teeming waters. This was the shimmering wealth from the wilderness, often called "New England's silvermine" and following the word of explorers since gone, fishermen had next become the ones who sailed this wretched shoreline and hoped

At the mouth of Boothbay Harbor, Burnt Island Light is a welcome sight to working lobstermen and vacationing windjammers alike.

Not to be confused with Ram Island Ledge Light in Casco Bay, the Ram Island Lighthouse is a more pastoral setting that attracts countless visitors to its Boothbay retreat.

to wrest some livelihood from its brine. Neither frightened by seas, nor fearful of work, these seamen toiled to reach New England with a purpose. If they knew it not before, then they learned this on the way: Atlantic winds blow hard here from the north, and loud and long they howl out in a storm. Riding heavy winds and rougher seas, they found that sometimes the voyage could be tedious; other times it could destroy their souls. Yet, they also had learned that the very coast which compromised the safety of all sailors also inveigled cod to spawn here during winter months when shallow bays were warmer than the deeper banks offshore. These early settlers were neither Pilgrims, nor Puritans, nor simply colonists; they were fishermen who came to do their business.

These men would be the first to change the landscape of this wilderness, but not with steeples peeking through the treetops. Instead, their seaside skyline rivaled that on shore. In fact, a good many new masts and spars had come from trees along these desolate shores; so, too, had hulls of boats that might be made with ordinary hand tools. With those, they were laying the keels of a rich New England heritage.

Hatchets and axes, handsaws and hammers, adzes and scrapers, chisels and mauls all along the shoreline rang a rhythm resounding in harmony that moved these native woods out to the New World's waters. Though the white pine belt ranged from the maritime regions the French had called "Arcadia" far down through western Maine and then New Hampshire, there stood timbers aplenty suitable for shaping. The short-needled trees the natives called "hackmatack" and which the English knew as junipers grew well in this primeval forest, along with chestnut and spruce, cedar and elm, as well as maple and oak. In time, they all took form as keels and ribs and stems, as well as decks and hulls. The first shapes were often as shallops and scows, local barges and longboats that easily maneuvered through the rivers, coves and marshes. Other craft were built for coastal travel, such as ketches and sloops.

But the greatest trees grew straight and tall, natural masts that Hudson discovered at Penobscot Bay in 1609. There and then, he stepped one as a foremast for his *Half Moon*, and a generation later the *Hercules* was bringing home the Old World's first cargo of masts out of New England. These would be the envy of shipmasters throughout the fleets of Europe. Yet, before any simple fisherman could afford to put together a fleet of his own that might move such products beyond this desolate coastline, the proprietors of these rich fisheries left the task of shipping their catch back home to the masters of those more seaworthy vessels, such as the *Hercules*, the *Fellowship*, the *Hunter*, and, of course, the *Angel Gabriel.*

On more than one occasion, the *Angel Gabriel* had made the fishing station at Richmond's Island a port of call off Cape Elizabeth. Her master knew Maine's waters, and he knew that there were some things to be reckoned with so close to the shore, regardless of a storm. He may not have known, however, just where he was when his *Angel Gabriel* was wrecked upon the ledges near Pemaquid. Nothing on the landfall signaled further hazards in the storm.

Nearly another 200 years would pass before Pemaquid Point would bear any lighthouse in 1827, though much sooner there would be some other lights in waters not so far away: Seguin Island off the Kennebec by 1795, Franklin Island Down East at Muscongus Bay by 1807, Burnt Island closer yet at Boothbay in 1821, and Monhegan Island by 1824. Still, none of these were built in time to do the master of the *Angel Gabriel* any good, just as the twin lights set at Thachers Island in 1771 did not exist in time to save those souls who met their final fate down there.

Despite the fishing and the coastal trades, yet another generation of sailors would be faced with dark New England shores before any ports might show any reliable light at all. Certainly, there were communities like that in Connecticut near Stratford Point at the mouth of the Housatonic River, where someone had almost always tried to keep a signal fire of sorts; however, the one which would find official sanction, and a keeper, came south of the entrance to Boston Harbor with a beacon on Point Allerton just off the beach at Hull. Busy Boston Harbor held the water and rocks that coursed along its glacial tributaries: the Chelsea and the Malden Rivers, the Island End and the Mystic Rivers, as well as the Neponset and the Charles.

"There are many small islands before Boston, well on to fifty, I believe, between which you sail on to the town," wrote the Dutchman Jaspar Dankers in his 1680 journal. "A high one, or the highest, is the first that you meet. It is twelve miles from the town and has a beacon upon it which you can see from a great distance, for it is in other respects naked and bare." On this rock-strewn headland was set the light of Point Allerton, commissioned by 1673 and at-

Closer to Europe than any other land in the United States, Maine was the coast toward which westbound voyagers set their courses, and Monhegan Island was often the landfall first seen. Even before the Monhegan Light was completed in 1824, the silhouette of the island's 200 foot elevation could be recognized almost 40 miles at sea.

tended to by Captain James Oliver.

Though it might have been little more than a lighted pole, it possibly resembled the vippefyr that was invented by Jens Pedersen Groves and first used along the Danish coast as early as 1624. Its design was very simple: across a high, set fulcrum point, a levered pole was placed. Upon one end of the lever was an open basket adequate for lighted coals; upon the other, a weight to help raise the glowing basket high, or lower it for stoking.

As primitive as the light at Point Allerton may have been, it did serve to some a promise; however, it would be years before a lighthouse changed the shape of skylines any further, for years would pass before any sort of trade within the colonies might justify the expense of putting up such lights. Though the beacon at Point Allerton may not have shone so brightly, it would stand out—much as had the pinnace *Virginia* and the pirate Dixey Bull—as a first along this darkened coast.

In the years before, the explorers and the colonists already had seen the need for such throughout New England's waters. In November of 1620, the master of the *Mayflower* had scuttled plans to skirt the shoals outside Cape Cod. Battered for 65 storm-tossed days at sea, pushed northward off course by an unknown force that others would later name the Gulf Stream, and sitting in tricky winds only some five miles off the Cape, Christopher Jones and his

Etching of Monhegan Island Light in Maine.

Mayflower soon faced conditions down off Monomoy that made him change his tack and seek protected waters.

These Pilgrims passed by shores where—in years to come—great beams of light would mark the way at Monomoy and Chatham, then north at the beach of Nauset, up to the highlands off Truro, and out to Provincetown's Race Point. Then, once inside the shelter of Cape Cod Bay, more lights would be around the shoreline at Provincetown's Wood End and closer by the harbor's mouth at Long Point.

But none of those existed as the *Mayflower* sought refuge at Provincetown before Master Jones decided to leave his passengers with little or no choice at Plimoth, a spot where the Indian Samoset had greeted them not long before he moved his own retinue a good distance north along the coastline to Pemaquid. "As one small candle can light a thousand," wrote Gov. Bradford in the years to follow, "so the light here kindled hath shone unto many, yea in some sort to a whole nation." His words might have been a portend of beacons and lighthouses yet to come; however, they eloquently described instead the tiny coastal plantation that alone remained in the dark of night. Despite its early settlement, Plymouth would remain without any lighthouse for another century and a half.

The primary purpose of a lighthouse, after all, was not simply to save the lives of sailors and of passengers. Its purpose was first to ensure the successful arrival of a merchant's shipment of goods, and these were something the simple settlers were certain not to have. In other settlements first, then, would some harbor lights appear to guide the way to safe passage into a more significant shipping port; other coastal lights would be set to mark a hazard or to distinguish an otherwise featureless landfall; and more than a few pairs of range lights would be placed in such a fashion that a pilot might verify his position in

At the approach to Boothbay Harbor, the Cuckolds was built originally in 1892 as a fog signal. When it was decided to convert the station into a lighthouse years later, the only space on the ledge for a lantern tower was atop the keeper's dwelling.

the middle of a channel by aligning one beacon directly in front of another. Most—if not all—of these would be built by merchants, at first, to save the ships and their cargoes. The value placed on these was more often than not far greater than any value that might have been placed on either the life, or the limbs of people aboard any vessel. After all, the master of a ship was the only one aboard who ever had any real direct connection with these monied men who dealt in commerce. Sometimes a part owner, the master of the ship was responsible for the navigation of the vessel and the conducting of any business during transit, as well as the safe transport and delivery of the cargo. Still, he was only one living soul, and if he cold not keep his ship afloat to deliver the goods, then he was of no greater use than any one of his subordinates might have been. In that little wooden world, everyone else seemed expendable.

Below the master ranked the mates, the carpenter, and an able seaman or two. Sometimes there were others, possibly ordinary seamen who were still literally learning the ropes, and none of them would be destined to become wealthy men; at least, not within legal bounds. Above them ranked the master, who often ruled with the temper of a tyrant; beneath them rolled the oceans of the world. As one old adage put it: "Those who would go to the sea for pleasure would go to hell for pastime." Seldom, if ever, did the wages match the task, but a good many sailors had nowhere else to work. Some had been taken

aboard against their very wishes, and others had sought some refuge from the law. In the eyes of the merchants, then, these souls were clearly a worthless lot. Certainly worth a lot less than any cargo or even the ship upon which they sailed. Any expenses paid out to build a lighthouse in the New World could only be justified in terms of the value of the goods. To the merchants, the darkness presented no mortal danger; the danger in the darkness could mean debt. The mooncussers underscored that, as did the colonial governments.

The highest on the Maine Coast, Seguin Island Light is also the only Maine lighthouse with a lens of the first order. The only other such lens in New England is located at Graves Light off Boston.

The members of this first group were nothing less than land pirates who did whatever they might to lure into shallows and onto the shores those ships richly burdened with goods. Without any lighthouse to warn of a danger, a master or sailor at sea might mistake a light along the coastline as either some indication of landfall, or else another ship with bearings more true. Too many times, however, it turned out to be the work of a group of mooncussers, so named because they cursed those nights when the light of the moon prevented their deadly deeds.

Sometimes they mounted a lantern atop a cattle yoke, then led the plodding beasts along the beach. Seen from a distance, this slowly moving light, pitching and yawling through the dark, might be viewed as a ship making deliberate headway. Other times, the mooncussers might place a light high on a pole, then stroll the shoreline just as slowly. Again, the illusion might be fulfilled, and

In contrast to the rockbound headlands of downeast Maine, or even the rising cliffs of the Great Outer Beach, the low, sandy Provincelands of Cape Cod drift into the nearby waters as they hook around Race Point, Wood End and Long Point.

a gullible, yet well-meaning master might be lured toward sure destruction. Once aground, his ship might be battered to pieces by breakers and his cargo washed into the shore. A few on the land might try to rescue the sailors, but more of them went for the goods.

In the 17th century, the colonies passed laws which required that any such shipwreck be reported immediately to the town clerk so that the ship and its cargo could be salvaged; however, there was more profit to be made in remaining mum. The promise of such silence then was allied to the darkness. So strong was the bond among them, that it has long been believed that mooncussers, wreckers, and the communities which found profit from their crimes did much in delaying the construction of needed lights as late as the mid-19th century. This belief was strong in the seaside villages throughout Cape Cod, Nantucket, Martha's Vineyard, and Long Island. Given the pace at which the lighthouse establishment grew, perhaps there is truth in that thought.

FIRST RAYS
OF HOPE

Even after they knew their needs, New Englanders did not invent the lighthouse any more than the Americans did. After all, the colonists who first established these beacons were subjects still loyal to someone's crown; however, even Englanders cannot be given credit for conceiving the lighthouse idea. Despite her pretensions of ruling the seas, as well as her legend of Eddystone Light, Britannia had built but a handful of lighthouses by the time that the Boston Light in her colony shone forth in 1716. Her archrival, France, had set up a few more than Britain, and so had the Dutch and Italians. Americans still tend to think first of their candle-shaped structures, white and alone on their coast of New England, whenever they think of a lighthouse.

Most authorities credit, however, the Egyptians with building the first lighthouse tower around 300 B.C. on the island of Pharos in the bay of Alexandria. There may well have been others before it, but no certain records exist. Homer made mention of lights on the mountains in his Iliad and Odyssey, but nowhere in documented history is there anything as significant before Pharos of Alexandria. Nor is there that much known about the lighthouse, other than the notation that the Egyptians dedicated this structure that held a place for a fire on its summit "for the safety of mariners." Once lighted, it stood for nearly a full millennium before going dark sometime after 700 A.D.; then, some 500 years after that, the entire structure crumbled in a Mediterranean earthquake.

The Greeks, as well, may have built a monumental lighthouse about the time that the Egyptians were building theirs. The great statue of Apollo, best known as the Colossus of Rhodes, is not only among the Seven Wonders of the Ancient World, but also is thought to have been a lighthouse of enormous magnitude, the same as the Pharos of Alexandria. Some have maintained that either in

Reconstructed after its ruin in the face of a New England storm, this newly-built Great Point Light on Nantucket is designed to last another full century.

Apollo's upraised hand, or else within his eyes, bright fires were burned to mark a way by the Aegean Sea. As did the Pharos of Alexandria, this colossus collapsed in an earthquake; however, it fell less than a century after its completion. Still, if the legacies of these two structures are looked upon as any indication of their original functions, then lighthouse aficionados must consider this:

the Colossus of Rhodes has lent its name to the root of those words which only indicate some enormous size; Pharos, on the other hand, has become the root for those words in several languages which can only apply to a lighthouse.

Semantics aside, history notes well that other lighthouse structures were built by Phoenicians and Romans throughout Spain, as well as France. By the time that the nations had developed any semblance of trade among one another, the number of lighthouses continued to increase through civilization's Dark and Middle Ages. Virtually any country which set a route upon the water marked its way along the shores with lights. The Turks, the Celts, the French, the Germans, and the British all worked with varying degrees of success to guarantee safe passage of their goods. By the early 18th century, New Englanders were trying to do that as well.

One by one, ports emerged through which merchants could ship their cargoes. Across New England and down to the other colonies, settlements continued to emerge along waters that provided access. Small and scattered communities, although not always trading or selling to others, nonetheless did need certain goods. Roads among them all were rough and rugged, too slow and much too difficult for moving merchandise. Almost naturally, then, the smaller boats that their local shipwrights made were employed for coastal trade among these tiny towns. Before long, the enterprising merchants with European ties

Among two of the handful of lights which grace the skyline of Boston Harbor are America's oldest lighthouse station, Boston Light, along with the stone tower of Graves Lighthouse in the distance. Clearly visible around Boston Light are the steel bands around the tower which help strengthen its shaft.

Though Sakonnet Point Light survived the awful Hurricane of 1938, its base had been damaged, and its condition further worsened with the force of Hurricane Carol in 1954. Rather than repair the light, however, the government abandoned the station, which now receives attention from the Friends of Sakonnet Light.

Once a pair of lights for mariners to easily distinguish, this southern tower of Thachers Island Light at Cape Ann now sets itself apart from many other Massachusetts lights by displaying a flashing beacon of red.

well understood the benefit of routing goods into and out of larger, central harbors, and so did nearby businessmen. After all, some guarantee of safe passage into a port would not only attract the seafaring ships, but also the coastal boats, as well as all the onshore spending that surrounds such activity.

Boston became the first of the colonies to mark the way to its harbor. Not far behind its progress with the light at Point Allerton, they set a tower upon one of the Brewster Islands at the easternmost edge of the harbor in 1716. The Boston merchants wanted it, but the entire Massachusetts colony paid for this "Light Hous and Lanthorn on some Head Land at the Entrance of the Harbor of Boston for the Direction of Ships and Vessels in the Night Time bound into the said Harbor." Eventually, shipping costs would compensate for the construction and maintenance. Seagoing vessels each paid a penny per ton for imports and exports; boats in the coastal trade paid only two shillings each time they left the harbor; and fishing boats paid even less, five shillings for a whole year. It seemed a sound investment, for the risks that still went with the shipping of goods were not unlike the folly forewarned in putting all of one's eggs in a single basket. So, in trying to move cargo both safely and swiftly, any sort of a lighthouse might surely be better than none at all.

The Boston Light was built much as the local boats had been, in that the local workmen used whatever tools and whatever materials were most readily at

hand. In this case, local stones and timbers were formed into the shape of a tapered tower: the higher the stone the better, to help keep it stable. Then it was topped with a lantern room that held either candles or lamps. When it was completed and lighted, New England had established the very first of America's lighthouses.

Though the official lighthouse of Mystic is at Latimer Reef, this photogenic tower within the harbor of Connecticut's historic seaport is a replica of Brant Point Light on Nantucket.

Between that time and the forming of a government for the United States of America in 1789, 12 more lighthouses would be built at other prospering ports throughout the colonies; two of those would follow the war for independence. Only the one at Sandy Hook, New Jersey to benefit New York merchants; another at Cape Henlopen, Delaware to help promote business in Philadelphia; a third at Morris Island in the harbor of Charleston, South Carolina; and quite possibly still one more upon Tybee Island in Savannah, Georgia were set outside New England waters. The wooden structure at Tybee Island was clearly constructed back then to serve as a landmark by day; however, uncertainty still exists as to whether or not it was equipped at that time to provide any beacon at night. Meanwhile, of the nine other lighthouses that stood within the colonies of New England, six had been built along the Massachusetts shore.

Still, most of the colonial coastline remained officially dark for yet another generation after the light was put up in Boston Harbor. Even before Nantucket townsfolk would construct their own beacon in 1746, Boston Light would al-

Just outside of Boston Harbor, the granite tower of Graves Light is patterned after the successful engineering designs of Minots Ledge Light at Cohasset Rocks, as well as the legendary Eddystone Light.

In order to build an offshore light, such as Southwest Ledge, engineers first constructed a ring of rip-rap, into the center of which they could submerge a cast-iron tube. After filling the tube with concrete, the workers constructed the tower upon that foundation.

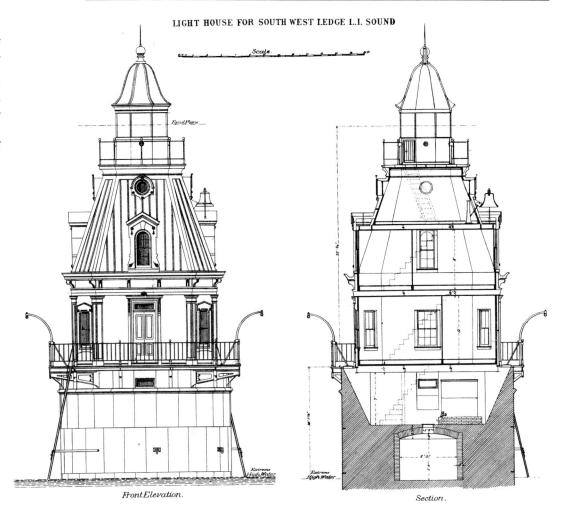

LIGHT HOUSE FOR SOUTH WEST LEDGE L.I. SOUND

Scale.

Focal Plane

Extreme High Water

Front Elevation.

Extreme High Water

Section.

ready undergo significant changes. For starters, there had been four different keepers, two of which drowned in Boston Light's first two years; the third keeper went on duty in November, 1718. Keeper John Hayes is the one who suggested that during the following year—at least on the side which faced out to the sea—some sort of a gallery ought to be built on the outside of the tower so that he might clear ice and snow from the lantern's glass. In addition, he said "That a great Gun may be placed on the Said Island to answer Ships in a Fogg." Both ideas were adopted for Boston Light.

When Nantucket finally set its light upon Brant Point at the entrance to the harbor on the protected, northern shore of the island, it was not an especially sophisticated station–a short wooden tower with its beacon on top. From the outset, Brant Point Light remained the responsibility of island ship owners who managed not only to propose the project at the town meeting on January 24, but also to have it completed by the scheduled gathering on April 28.

Two lights then marked New England's coast, but many a danger still lingered. After all, the entire Down East coast of Maine sat lurking in the darkness, as did the reefs and ledges of Long Island Sound. Among them all still stretched the shallow, shifting Cape Cod shores. There were other hazards, too, from Cape Cod north to Boston and then from Cape Ann's rocky shore toward Maine. Two lights did not a safe world make, and few things were any more treacherous to a ship than what was waiting southward off Nantucket. In time, the shipping world would come to refer to the area simply as "The Cross-

roads" where ships from Europe, Canada, New York, Norfolk, Baltimore, and Philadelphia would pass each other in search of their own destinations.

Not unlike the open Atlantic, this area south of Cape Cod and the islands remained a vast and trackless ocean. Yet, here among the likelihood of a growing number of vessels, sat a somewhat greater hazard in the form of inscrutable fog. Perhaps one of the foggiest areas along the entire Eastern seaboard, the dirty weather and congested shipping of The Crossroads threatened to turn this particular spot on every master's chart into a dreaded graveyard of ships.

Already, the darkness and the fog had become responsible for the death of many a ship that had tried to sail past Cape Cod's Great Outer Beach; The Crossroads proved a rival to that claim, for never did the area ever provide what anyone might term "ideal" shipping weather. Calm, clear days were few. When the weather was clear, the seas would be rough. When the air was calm, the fog would set in with its close and lasting blanket that folded tight against the cold Atlantic seas.

Shipmasters had another route, although it still proved tricky. To avoid The Crossroads they might navigate the shallowed rip between Monomoy Point on Cape Cod and Great Point on Nantucket. Once through, they could past westerly into shallow, but protected waters: first Nantucket Sound, into Vineyard Sound, then across Block Island Sound, and on through Long Island Sound,

High above the crumbling, sandy headlands of the Great Outer Beach of Cape Cod, Nauset Light is no longer a station of three towers easily identifiable far out at sea. Instead, its beacons flash first red, then white, and its tower is painted with a distinctive band of crimson.

Rebuilt about the time that Watch Hill was constructed, the four-sided tower at Beavertail Light replaced the last vestiges of the original, which is considered the third lighthouse station built in New England.

down to the mouth of the Hudson. In years to come, lighthouses and lightships would show the way. Meanwhile the route remained touch and go.

Not long after Brant Point Lighthouse had been built, the General Assembly of the English Colony of Rhode Island and the Providence Plantation set their own four-cornered, rubblestone tower at the southern tip of Conanticut Island in 1749. King George's War had ended against France and Spain only the year before, and during those years of hostility privateers out of Newport and Bristol were sailing these waters alongside the ships of both smugglers and merchants who traded for slaves and molasses. When the war at last ended with the Treaty of Aix-la-Chapelle, the British would hold title to most of Canada, and the French would be left with Cape Breton Down East, where they spent vast sums of money to build upon the southern coast at Louisbourg an almighty

fortress as strong as Gibraltar. There, too, in 1733 they had built the first of all Canada's lights, the second in all the New World.

In peacetime, then, Beavertail Lighthouse was lighted to mark the cliffs between the Western Passage and the Eastern Passage of Narragansett Bay, where it might show the way for mariners into Newport Harbor, then further north toward Bristol, then on up into Providence.

Before the next New England lighthouse would be completed, however, fire—an always present lighthouse danger right up until very recent years—would greatly damage the original two structures that had stood at Boston and Brant Point. In 1751, flames gutted the rubble Boston Light of all its wooden parts, especially its staircase and its decks, so while repairs were made a temporary beacon was set atop a spar not very far away. A similar fate befell the Brant Point Light in 1758; however, the next one built would be only the second of perhaps as many as nine reincarnations of the original tower that had been placed on Brant Point. Even today, its reputation as being the lowest-level lighthouse in New England stands alongside its reputation as the one New England lighthouse that has most often been reconstructed.

West of the Beavertail Lighthouse and on into Long Island Sound, the New London Lighthouse was built at the mouth of the Thames River in Connecticut in 1760. Neither names at this port were always so. In 1652, six years after John

The last of the Rhode Island lighthouses to be manned, the station at Block Island Southeast beams a flashing green beacon more than 200 feet above the nearby Atlantic. It is New England's only primary seacoast with a light of that color.

Winthrop had founded a settlement there at Nameaug along the Monhegin, the settlers still yearned for what they considered a more civilized name, so they were granted permission to use the names of both the land and the river from where they had come.

From New London on the Thames they launched their boats to trade furs and skins for whatever goods they might need in other ports from Maine to the Virginia. The shipping trade grew, as did a fledgling whaling industry; however, the hazards of rocks and reefs simply grew worse with the increase in water traffic. So, merchants and townsfolk alike agreed that a lighthouse might decrease the danger, and they convinced the General Assembly of the Colony of Connecticut to fund the project with a lottery, as well as a tax on shipping. The original lighthouse at New London Harbor was a simple cylindrical tower made of stone that served the colonies as the fourth light in their simple system. Not long after in 1764, the Sandy Hook Lighthouse was constructed south and west of Long Island Sound, and three years after that, both the Delaware Lighthouse at Cape Henlopen and the Charleston Light on Morris Island were built to light those waters. For almost a decade, then, no new lighthouses were built along New England's coast. The next, however, would come in 1769 upon Gurnet Point in Plymouth, not too many miles south of Boston and on the western shore of Cape Cod Bay. Unlike the other stations that showed some kind of

tower structure, the lighthouse at the Gurnet first was truly more a house in shape. Not especially large, the squat rectangular building atop the northern entrance to Plymouth Bay was as tall as it was long, measuring 20 feet in both directions and sitting 15 feet wide. At each end of the roof was a lantern, neither of which had lamps that shone with any remarkable brilliance. It was, nonetheless, a lighthouse.

The next two stations were built to the north of Boston in 1771. One was actually a set of twin lights upon Thachers Island at Cape Ann; the other, a single tower beside Fort William and Mary on Newcastle Island by the mouth of the harbor in Portsmouth, New Hampshire. The 80 or so acres which constitute Thachers Island at the western headlands are not that much different from the site of the nation's original lighthouse at Point Allerton. Basically, huge boulders abound among the lower course of shoreline gravel, but high upon this rocky headland two towers were built some 300 yards apart. Each was only 45 feet tall, but the island's height had made their lanterns stand at nearly 90 feet above the sea around them. From that height, the beams might be visible as far as 16 miles at sea, sufficient to guide a ship and keep its hull from danger.

Not far to the north, in the shadow of Mount Agamenticus, the mouth of the Piscataqua River holds a harbor, broad and deep. The only seaport in New Hampshire, Portsmouth was kept clear of most ice in the winter by Pis-

Not too far east of New Hampshire's Newcastle Light at the mouth of Piscataqua River sits Whaleback Light (pictured low to the right), which is in Maine's territorial waters. To the north is an abandoned lifesaving station, and leagues beyond is the Isle of Shoals Light.

Aside from having fallen to unsightly disrepair, the rusted tower and aged dwelling of Monomoy Point Light had become further back from the water's edge than where it once stood; however, the lighthouse station had not moved. Instead, the drifting sands had altered the shoreline around it.

cataqua's hard-running tide; as well, she could be reckoned from afar by the height of the peak just behind her. Only at night might she be otherwise passed without notice. So, there a wooden tower was built upon Fort Point.

Just northeast from this shore, but truly in the waters that belong to Kittery, Maine, sits Whaleback Island, so named for the dark shape of its ledge. In time, that spot would also hold a lighthouse of its own, as would White Island in the Isle of Shoals some three leagues further distant out to sea. So short is the shoreline of New Hampshire when compared to all of New England's, that many tend to overlook these two coastal lights which rightly are her own. Inland stand three more upon Lake Sunapee at Burkehaven, Loon Island, and Herrick Cove. These, however, were not erected until the late 19th century. During the infancy of the lighthouse system, however, New Hampshire could boast of at least one light that stood at the entrance to Portsmouth Harbor.

These 11 original lighthouses were all in place at the outset of the Revolutionary War, which came to a head when the British tried to control the commerce of the colonies in favor of the mother country. At Brant Point Light on Nantucket Island, where its people and the British had agreed to a separate peace, the tower rebuilt in 1759 blew over in 1774; at Beavertail in Rhode Island, the British torched the lighthouse; at Boston Light, colonial troops dismantled the lantern in 1775 so that it could not aid the British, and the redcoats responded

by blowing it up altogether in 1776; at the Plymouth Light, a ball from a cannon in an offshore skirmish landed on the light, but never diminished the lantern; at Portsmouth Light, John Paul Jones took over command of the Ranger in 1777; at Thachers Island, the towers were made to fall dark when Minute Men chased off the original keeper, who was found to be a Tory; only at New London, did the lighthouse remain unscathed, a beacon to guide to safety roving privateers.

The year after the war was over, Massachusetts built two more lighthouses on her own. One was placed in 1784 across the water from Monomoy Island at Great Point on nearby Nantucket. From there, the beacon could guide ships safely past the rips and shoals into Nantucket Sound. Another lighthouse was built north of Cape Ann on Plum Island at the mouth of the Merrimack River to mark the entrance to Newburyport Harbor. Commissioned in 1788, this would be the last of the lighthouses before the new federal government took over their administration.

Still commonly known as Two Lights, Maine's Cape Elizabeth Light was once the eastern tower of the pair which marked this landfall south of Portland; however, the lantern on the western tower was dismantled in 1924 when the government converted all lighthouse stations into single beacons.

CANDLES IN THE WIND

In wintertime, this raw New England coast can seem to be a single element as sea and shore together share a less than friendly hue. Sometimes the northeastern granite shows its hard sepulchral face of grays all cracked with shadows holding onto snow, while winds blast past the grim-visaged sea that nudges at its side. No less somber than the stone's sullen crags, the water insists on its own leaden look, tempered at times by a brief flash of sunlight and crested on high with white foam.

Other days in winter, this same locale may just as soon seem innocent, quiet and still beneath a new fallen snow that has drifted on beaches, settled on boulders, and blanketed bays bound by ice. For a while, at least, nothing might ever seem able to move, but little has been changed underneath, where ledges and shallows and reefs seen in summer still threaten all hulls that sail near. Even in moments of unblemished beauty, each sight by itself could give shivers to sailors who moved through these waters with canvas and wood.

All in all at the threshold of the 19th century, there were far more rugged sites such as these along the ragged edge of New England than any ship's master might ever avoid, and each would approach them with fear in his heart. These were not sailors beguiled by such beauty or lured by dame Nature's more sirenesque charms; however, often they found themselves suddenly here and wanting to be someplace else. Many more years would pass before most such dangers along these hostile shores could be properly posted, marked with a warning that alerted all ships of the perils awaiting nearby. Until there was any central authority to determine these threats, to recommend the building of some sort of lighthouse, and to pay for the efforts involved, most of the beacons along this horizon England remained the projects of commercial in-

The Spring Point Ledge Light was built in 1897 on the breakwater at Portland Harbor. Like Maine's Goose Rocks Light, Connecticut's Peck Ledge and Greens Ledge Lights, Rhode Island's Sakonnet Point, Plum Beach and Conimicut Lights, and several others commissioned in the late 19th century, this tower was a pre-fabricated cone of cast iron designed to reduce contruction costs in marking underwater hazards.

Reflected in a pool of its surrounding granite ledge is the lantern of Portland Head, which was automated during ceremonies on August 9, 1989 to mark the bicentennial celebration of the United States lighthouse system.

terests hoping to attract ships into one budding port or another.

With the government of the United States of America at last beginning to take on some shape, however, the responsibility for building and maintaining lighthouses, as well as all other aids to navigation, finally held out the promise of some uniformity. In 1789, each of the local communities and colonies which had built the original lighthouses of New England gave up control to those existing ones, along with the control over the others then being built at places such as Newburyport in Massachusetts and Portland Head in what would eventually become the state of Maine. Viewed as part of shipping and commerce, these and all other lighthouse stations would be overseen by the Department of the Treasury for more than the next hundred years.

At first, they were personally administered by Alexander Hamilton before he relinquished control in 1792 to the commissioner of revenue, whose responsibilities included the collection of customs fees at every port. Even then, with the inclusion of a new lighthouse at Virginia's Cape Henry upon the Chesapeake that year, as well as the addition of a lantern atop the longstanding tower at Tybee Island in Savannah, these lighthouses numbered only 15. For almost the next 30 years, the control of the lighthouse system passed back and forth between the commissioners of revenue and the secretaries of the treasury, until the superintendency of all the lighthouses fell at last in 1820 to the

office of the fifth auditor of the treasury.

By that time, the War of 1812 had been waged by this young nation against Britain, partly in pursuit of neutral shipping rights for American vessels, while France and England engaged in hostilities of their own. By then, too, the number of lighthouses had increased dramatically to include at least 30 others throughout New England waters: from West Quoddy Head in Lubec, Maine, down through Annisquam Harbor in Gloucester, Massachusetts, past Watch Hill, Rhode Island, and along Long Island Sound at places like Connecticut's Black Rock Harbor.

Even back then, the idea of a canal cutting through Cape Cod to spare every master the torment of the treacherous trip around the peninsula remained little more than a seaman's pipe dream. In fact, the busiest waters in all the world beyond the English Channel were then within the New England sounds, already bounded by the lighthouse stations at Cape Pogue on Chappaquiddick Island on the eastern end of Martha's Vineyard; at West Chop not far away in Holmes Hole, later known as Vineyard Haven; at Tarpaulin Cove on Naushon Island in the group that Gosnold had named the Elizabeths; at Gay Head on the western end of the Vineyard; at Point Judith and Watch Hill, both south and west of Beavertail Lighthouse in Rhode Island; and down at Montauk Point on the easternmost tip of Long Island. Vessels heading east and north through Nantucket

Set on Wigwam Point, the Annisquam Light is the oldest of the four Massachusetts lighthouse stations that have marked the Gloucester peninsula.

Originally commissioned in 1808, Watch Hill Light in the southwestern corner of Rhode Island was rebuilt just before the Civil War with a rectangular brick tower, 10 feet square and 45 feet high. Overlooking Fishers Island Sound, the Watch Hill station looks very much like its Beavertail counterpart, not far across Rhode Island's waters; however, is stands much closer to the light on Long Island's Montauk Point only 14 miles away.

Sound would drop anchor off the Vineyard to await the most favorable weather conditions; ships heading toward the other direction would gain added speed by riding the tides and the currents through Block Island Sound, on into Long Island Sound.

So, there all the lights were indeed keenly watched, and poor lights could cost someone dearly. In short, the safe passage for most of the commerce surrounding this young nation fell primarily to the office of an assiduous book-keeper named Stephen Pleasonton, who had accepted—along with his more customary clerical tasks—control over these aids to navigation. Unfortunately, his overriding concern for economics would reign for more than 30 years.

Represented at the local levels by the collectors of customs, who often held their own local titles as superintendents of lights, Pleasonton provided rather strict, unimaginative guidelines. These allowed his subordinates to administer virtually every local matter that might arise, whether that was choosing light-house sites and buying land, or issuing construction contracts, then overseeing the work. Though the secretary of the treasury officially appointed every light-house keeper, they, too, were generally picked by the local people.

Even so, the secretary of the treasury seldom had any more knowledge of their qualifications, or of lighthouse technology, or even of simple station maintenance than did the fifth auditor, who seemed more often than not to possess

no such knowledge whatsoever. In fact, the closest administrative associate with any understanding remotely related to such maritime matters was a retired captain named Winslow Lewis, himself a Cape Cod native from Wellfleet. His affiliation with Pleasanton is said to have hindered the whole operation of the lighthouse system much more than it ever helped. The fifth auditor, meanwhile, remained little more than a diligent clerk who accepted the word of his local collectors, each of whom received as a salary a percentage of whatever money might be spent upon the lighthouses within their separate jurisdictions.

Hovering over a cliff that towers nearly a hundred feet above Penobscot Bay peers the lighthouse from Owls Head. Some claim the name of the land was derived from the outcrop of granite whose shape resembles the wise old bird; others say the Indians named it so.

That is not to say that others did feel more noble obligations. Sometimes sailing and occasionally trekking to these often unreachable extremes of the land, they sought to place their daymarks and their beacons in places other than at the mouths of harbors. At the western end of Muscle Ridge Channel off the coast of Maine, for example, Whitehead Light had been built in 1804. Still another generation would pass before the eastern end of the channel might be marked in 1826 by the light at Owls Head, but Whitehead had hosted some greater problems, namely fog.

Once a favored anchorage along the busiest waters outside of the English Channel, the lighthouse at Tarpaulin Cove stands on the island of Naushon, low among the Elizabeths, west by southwest of Cape Cod.

More than any other point along the coast of Maine, Whitehead was notorious for its dirty weather, averaging in most years more than twice as many hours of fog than ever recorded at any other place. Though the lighthouse at West Quoddy Head was built a year later at the easternmost point of the conti-

Squatting atop its snow-covered perch, the relatively short tower of Owls Head Light holds a lantern than remains a full 100 feet above sea level.

nental United States, that later station was provided in 1820 with the very first fog bell in the nation, and Whitehead would wait until 1837.

Meanwhile, Whitehead also exemplified some of the weaknesses of the young system. Only two years after the station had been commissioned, Keeper Ellis Dolph was discovered selling the lighthouse oil to others for a profit in 1807. Six years later, Winslow Lewis discovered that Keeper Ebeneezer Otis was too sickly a person to maintain the light. Nevertheless, Otis was kept at the post until his death some three years later.

Despite such examples of dubious distinction, though, there appeared at several other locations, such as Franklin Island off the coast of Maine and Little Gull Island in Long Island Sound, newly-chosen locations for New England's lighthouses. The areas were so remote that no one had yet chosen to settle there. That meant that a lighthouse would have to be built either from nearby wood or stone, or else from whatever materials might be shipped or hauled away into this coastal wilderness.

As had been the case in building ships, the people did the best that they could in applying their skills to whatever materials were available. Since the building of the first beacon upon Point Allerton and then the tower in Boston Harbor, the differences down through the years among construction techniques, as well as among lighthouse designs, closely followed the other evolu-

tions within the nation's growth. So, America's lighthouse system of sorts continued to flourish throughout New England, with the work of those who built towers of wood where they had to, or rubble where they had it, and then granite when they had found they could move it.

Still, regardless of whether such towers would be built out of wood or of rubble, out of granite or of brick, or—in years still to come—out of concrete or iron pre-cast, the concern among mariners had always remained from the first that the light should be clearly visible. This demanded particular attention to two factors: that the lighthouse be high enough for its lantern to be seen as far as it might out to sea, and that the lighthouse be strong enough not be toppled easily by water or by wind. These concerns of the mariners, though, were not always foremost among Pleasonton, Lewis, and others beneath them, whose untimely practice of politics did often endanger the safety of ships and the lives of sailors at sea.

It took, perhaps, a full generation of their questionable policies to reveal any possible pattern of political problems. By 1838 the Congress had become somewhat suspicious as to whether or not the Treasury Department's siting of lighthouses, along with its budgeting, bidding, and spending procedures, were serving the best interests of America's commerce. Since the start of the Pleasonton superintendency, yet another 43 lighthouses had been built along New

Beyond the lantern room of Gay Head Light at the western end of Martha's Vineyard, the waters of Vineyard Sound, Buzzards Bay, and Rhode Island Sound converge into fast-moving tidal waters. Beneath the watch of this squatting tower, most of America's commerce once moved.

England's waters, providing this stretch of northeast coastline with nearly half of all the nation's lighthouse stations. Despite that growth—or perhaps because of it—the Congress asked that the Navy Department inspect each of the nation's lights. Among the conclusions of that investigation was the disturbing condition of many lighthouse structures, let alone their lanterns.

Along the Connecticut shoreline, for example, the stone tower at Black Rock Harbor was being shored up with timbers, while not so far away at Greenwich, the mortar had yet to dry in the tower on Great Captain Island. The one at Black Rock had been built in 1809, then built again after the gale of 1824. The other, at Great Captain, had been built little more than a decade before the Navy inspectors had come to pay their visit.

Out on Cape Cod, the twin towers built at Chatham Harbor in 1808 were also typical of several problems that stemmed from local oversight. The first problem was a matter of construction. Planned and designed as two towers of stone, both had instead been built out of wood because no one could find enough suitable stones along the outer Cape to follow the contract as signed. Wood, on the other hand, was plentiful for two such towers.

The second problem was simply a matter of numbers. There were two towers built at Chatham Harbor to prevent a single tower from being mistaken for the one which represented Cape Cod Light, which was not too far north along

the same Great Outer Beach. The two towers at the Chatham station were not unique, for there were already twin towers built on Thachers Island at Cape Ann, as well as twin towers at Bakers Island in Salem Harbor. In Maine, other sets would be constructed on Matinicus Rock in 1827, then at Cape Elizabeth two years later.

This multiple tower situation, however, finally reached a point worth questioning on Cape Cod when the three towers of Nauset Beach Light were aligned only 150 feet apart. Situated in the town of Eastham, between Truro and Chatham, the "Three Sisters" were meant to avoid being confused with the Cape Cod Light to their north, and the twin lights of Chatham Harbor to the south. And though it may have been another instance where some local mind had found that there was a profit in such a duplicate plan, the Navy inspector thought it was a clear case of "overlighting."

If both quality and quantity of lighthouse towers were the first of two problems which Chatham Harbor typified, then the third was nothing less than another case of someone's poor judgment–this time in the matter of siting. The merciless Atlantic devoured the coastline from under the towers and forced their eventual relocation back from the precipice by 1878. That had already happened at the Cape Cod Light at Truro, when the original 30 foot tower built in 1797 was replaced altogether less than 50 years later with the one which to

Just above the entrance to Vineyard Haven, the cast-iron tower of East Chop Light displays traces of its Victorian heritage in the molding around its windows, as well as the braces supporting the lantern's gallery. Privately maintained until 1873, when the government finally took responsibility almost a century after it had taken on the others, East Chop Long displayed a green beacon that could be seen some 15 miles at sea.

Warning ships that ply the waters where Narragansett Bay and Long Island Sound wash together, the first tower for this Rhode Island lighthouse was built in 1810 to mark the Point Judith Harbor of Refuge.

this day stands more than 60 feet above the ground. Again, the problem had not been so much the construction of the earlier tower as it was the selection of the original site, which was too close to the cliffs that hung above the surf.

In fact, the majestic tower that is Cape Cod Light, much as those in Boston Harbor, at Portland Head and Sankaty Head, along with the one at Montauk Point, serves well as a model of a coastal light's tower construction. From the top of its cap to the mark of mean low tide on the Great Outer Beach below, the full height above sea level is nearly a 160 feet. This is sufficient to allow its beacon to be seen far enough at sea to prevent mariners from stranding their vessels along the shifting shoals. It was that specific distance beyond the Cape's particular dangers which helped determine the height of Cape Cod Light.

Lighthouse engineers call this distance at sea the geographic range of the light. That is the visibility which the curvature of the earth will allow between the light itself and the eye of an observer out beyond the danger. At the time of the building of the second tower, an observer was considered to be on a ship's deck some 15 feet above the water. Today, he is considered to be on a ship's bridge, another 25 feet higher.

High enough up to be seen and now far enough back to be safe from the seas, Cape Cod Light also retained a familiar form. While some lighthouse towers in New England were built with four sides such as the one at Beavertail Light in Rhode Island, or at Hospital Point north of Boston, or at Two Bush Light in Maine—and then others came to reflect the industrialized progress of cast-iron caissons—such as those at Latimer Reef in Mystic, Connecticut, or at Butler Flats just off New Bedford, or at Spring Point Ledge in Portland, Maine—the classical shape of Cape Cod Light is one which seems to be something more traditional. When it was first built, however, this design was just coming into use throughout the world, while earlier New England towers had consisted of as many as six or eight flattened sides.

Like many others, though, Cape Cod Light had a shape that was rounded to best withstand the winds and waters from whatever quadrant of the compass, and its base was widest to provide support. At the bottom of Cape Cod Light,

Though the original twin towers of Matinicus Rock Light were built of wood in 1827, they were replaced with granite shafts in 1848. When the government consolidated all such lighthouses into stations with single beacons in 1924, the northern tower was dismantled.

The first lighthouse to be completed under the direction of the new government of the United States of America was also Maine's very first: Portland Head.

Once the beacon which sailors all sought as their first American landfall, the automated station at Cape Cod Light now sends forth a coded radio signal, as well as its traditional beacon of light.

the walls of brick are 3 feet thick, but hollow within to provide some insulation from the seasonal extremes of the New England weather. The temperature inside was often more critical for the proper maintaining of the oil than it was for the comfort of the keeper, who accepted with the job the fact that he might be most busy when the weather was at its worst. However, most towers were built with the keeper's access in mind.

This structure was just the tower; however, there often were other buildings: an oil shed, sometimes a boathouse, and usually a dwelling of some sort. On occasion, however, the keeper found shelter within the tower itself. Perhaps the most poignant, as well as the most frightful of any episode involving such a structure, is Minots Ledge. Located offshore in the reefs just south of Boston off Cohasset, some have called it the nation's most dangerous lighthouse.

Partially as a result of the congressional investigation in 1838, a lighthouse was proposed for this general area. Almost 10 years later a specific recommendation was made by the Topographical Department that an iron pile lighthouse be set upon Minots Rock. It was the best site off Cohasset, but it was not an especially good one. For about three hours during low tide, an area only some 25 feet wide appeared above the water, and upon that Stephen Pleasonton would allow the construction of this relatively new style tower. The prevailing thought was that the forces of water would meet with less resistance from a set

of narrow iron piles than from broad surface of stone.

The proposed design follows. Set in holes drilled 5 feet into the rock would be nine iron piles, eight of these legs would be around the 25 foot perimeter, and the ninth would be in the center. Cemented into the rock, these eight legs would be braced around the outside, as well as to the ninth leg in the center. Atop them all would be placed the lantern; below that would be the keeper's quarters; and below them both, a supply deck nearly 70 feet above sea level. The project took nearly three years to finish, and when it was finally lighted on January 1, 1850, Minots Ledge tower was the first one in America that was fully exposed to the powers of the Atlantic Ocean.

By April of that year, Keeper Isaac Dunham and his assistants had experienced enough racking and straining at the mercy of the New England weather to implore the government to strengthen the tower. However, nothing was done, and Dunham resigned in October. The new keeper was John Bennett. He not only suffered similar tossings as late into the following year as April, but also forwarded similar complaints to the fifth auditor's office. An investigation was made, but the government did nothing more.

Then another storm blew into New England on April 16, 1851. When at last the fury subsided, the Minots Light was gone, reduced to twisted knot of iron stumps embedded in the ledge off Cohasset. With the lighthouse had perished

Across the low-lying heathlands of North Truro, the prevailing winds allow only two things to rise up. One is the stunted growth of scrub pines; the other, Cape Cod Light.

The notorious lighthouse at Minots Ledge displays itself somewhat ominously above these infamous waters of the Bay State.

Despite its name, the island that sits beneath Two Bush Light nurtures neither trees, nor bushes. At one time its landscape included two lone pines; now its skyline is the solitary lighthouse.

For years, Heron Neck Light has stood on Green Island; however, in 1989 the island's owner renamed the property to honor the President of the United States, who claims ties to Maine. Now, Heron Neck Light on Bush Island should not be confused with Two Bush Light.

the keeper's two assistants. Not too many months after that tragedy, gone as well would be the authority of the fifth auditor over the growing system of lighthouses. In 1852, a nine-member Lighthouse Board was created, and its authority matched its expertise. Among its earliest recommendations was the one which designated a more conventional stone tower for Minots Ledge.

The new project lasted most than five years, from June of 1855 to August of 1860, and it patterned the tower after principles gleaned from lessons learned at England's famed Eddystone Light. The first 40 feet of granite courses, dovetailed and interlocked, provided a solid foundation. The next 40 feet was enough for a storage space, a keeper's quarters, and the lantern house. A similar design would be applied in years to come at the lighthouse that sat on the ledge known as Bishops & Clerks, just offshore Cape Cod in Nantucket Sound. Despite their structural innovations, these water bound towers retained the conical shape which most still identify as being their idea of a lighthouse.

True, they might not have been the pure, white structures that most people have come to identify with a lighthouse and its good intentions, but they still served their essential purpose. Even those brown or gray stone towers, which did not stand-out as whitewashed daymarks along the bleak New England shoreline, still displayed recognizable characteristics of their own. Many were given identifiable bands of brilliant red, such as those at West Quoddy Head,

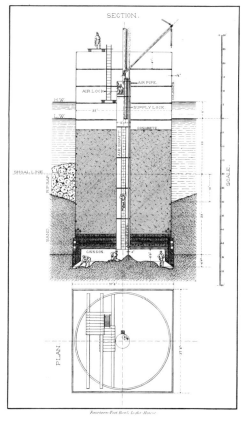

SECTION.

AIR LOCK

AIR PIPE.

H.W

L.W

SUPPLY LOCK

CONCRETE

SHOAL LINE

RIP RAP

SAND

CAISSON.

SCALE

PLAN

Fourteen-Foot Bank Light-House

In the late 19th century, engineering of offshore lighthouse foundations progressed from the masonry of stations such as Race Rock, to the iron caissons of Southwest Ledge, then on to the pneumatic caisson foundation. With this advancement, the cast-iron caisson was filled with concrete, except for a central airshaft. Using this airlock, workers could climb to the bottom and continue excavation until the foundation had settled to the determined depth. Once the work was complete, the remaining space would also be filled with concrete.

Protected by hollowed walls that measure up to 3 feet thick, the spiraling staircase of Cape Cod Light winds toward the deck just beneath the lantern room.

Built in 1858, the original brick tower of Bass Harbor Head continues to cast its beacon across this Maine harbor and Blue Hill Bay.

Nauset Beach, and Sankaty Head.

Somewhat less quick to be noticed by those on the land as a lighthouse design, but nonetheless still quite wonderful themselves, were the grandiose dwellings of masonry that adorned the New England coastlines south and west of Massachusetts. The keeper's dwelling was made of brick, or of clapboard that sometimes supported the lantern on top, which was the case at such stations as St. Croix River Light in Maine, Bass River Light on Cape Cod, and the original lighthouse at Edgartown Harbor on Martha's Vineyard. Eventually, masonry of red brick, fieldstone, and granite were used at Block Island North Light in Rhode Island, New London Ledge Light in Connecticut, and Race Rock Light in Fishers Island Sound. The same was also true of the majestic structure adorning Vermont's Colchester Reef in the waters of Lake Champlain.

In time it didn't matter whether a New England lighthouse looked like a whitewashed cone or a topless pyramid, whether a keeper's dwelling was made of wooden clapboard or roughened fieldstone, or whether a roof was trimmed with Victorian scrollwork or tiled with a Mansard slant. The form was not of the utmost importance, just as long as it stood up to the elements. After all, what mattered most to the sailor at sea was not the house, but the light.

PILLARS
OF FIRE

Light has always been invested by mankind with powers much greater than its basic physical properties. The Greeks told stories not only of the Titan Prometheus, who first stole fire from the gods to benefit the mortals, but also of the virtuous Diogenes, who carried his lantern throughout the streets in search of an honest man. In countless civilizations across further generations since, the presence of light has come to symbolize the triumph of knowledge over ignorance, the triumph of love over hate, and essentially the triumph of everything good over evil. Most still believe, after all, that it is better to light one small candle than to curse the darkness. In the case of a coastal lighthouse, truer thoughts were never held, for this particular pillar of fire came to symbolize the triumph of safety over danger, and the mere sighting of a lighthouse from land or from sea still can kindle a spark of emotion.

Throughout the entire history of these coastal lights, nearly every keeper has had to concern himself with a flame of one sort or another. In the earliest of times, the lights were little more than wood-burning fires upon the beach, or else baskets of coals hung on poles. Next came those fires set high up on hills; then wood fires placed atop towers. Aside from the fact that all this open flame allowed the actual rays of lights to escape aimlessly above and uncontrollably across the darkness of the night, these wood fires also required throughout the night a constant stoking by the keepers.

As nearby wood supplies around the lighthouse towers vanished when the trees were virtually depleted, first coal and then oil became the major sources of fuel for lighthouse lamps. Not only did coal provide a brighter, steadier glow which was more visible far out at sea, but it also demanded less attention by the keeper. All too often, though, the keepers would abandon the coals for the

Designed more in the style of the early Cape Cod lights than in the fashion of others Down East, the lighthouse at Egg Rock was built with its lantern tower on the roof of the keeper's dwelling.

evening, only to wake up and discover that their glowing heat had burned through their iron grates. In addition, coal and oil both produced a dimming soot that kept the keepers busy cleaning the glass surrounding the lantern.

Candles held some advantages, but even the invention of the electric light was slow in making its way to the lantern room. After all, most lighthouses had been built so remotely distant from any sources of electrical power that a controllable flame remained the one type of lantern available. Only in the early 1930s, for example, did the Cape Cod Light change from its original source of light–oil-burning lamps.

When the stations at Cape Cod and Montauk were both commissioned in 1797, the light each gave off was from a lantern room of spider lamps. These were little more than shallow pans of whale oil, each containing four solid, tubular wicks without any chimneys. Simple as these were, they caused a mess, because the spider lamps gave off a pungent smoke that not only soiled the lantern glass throughout the tower, but also prevented the keeper from staying very long within the lantern room to clean them.

Not long after the Cape Cod Light had been built, mariners began to report that they often had difficulty telling the difference between the Boston Light and this newer light to the south on Truro's High Lands. Only a few years earlier, the federal lighthouse legislation passed in 1792 had made it law that, "The

light in the lighthouse shall be such as to distinguish it from others and prevent mistakes." So later, when a civil engineer reported to the government that there was "no way of telling one light from another on dark nights" and that there was "no accurate method of comparing intensity of one light to another, such as listing candlepower," the Cape Cod Light was fitted with a mechanical eclipser in 1800.

Across the foggy moors of Nantucket Island, the beacon of Sankaty Head Light appears to rise amidst the heathers, but it actually stands on a sandy cliff far above the vast Atlantic.

Revolving slowly around the the lantern, this consisted of a semi-circular screen which blocked out a portion of the light as it completed a rotation every eight minutes. The result at sea was the effect of a flashing beacon, the first in any American lighthouse. By 1807, however, the eclipser was removed after an inspector determined that too much of the light's intensity was being diminished; the luminous range was being impaired for most of the time.

Meanwhile, within the next few years in England and in Europe, lighthouses were outfitted with a lamp invented by Aime Argand in 1781. Using a hollow tubular wick inside a glass chimney, the Argand lamp allowed oxygen not only to flow along both the inside and the outside of the wick, but also to burn with a brighter, smokeless flame that had the intensity of seven candles. When backed with a reflector shaped like a parabola, each Argand lamp could produce a light that was even four hundred times that brightness, the brightest lighthouse lanterns in the world.

Built on Turtle Hill in 1797, the sandstone tower of Long Island's Montauk Light has often been the first land-fall—and tragically, some-times the last—that count-less voyagers into and out of New England waters have witnessed for nearly 200 years.

Etching of Montauk Light.

Unfortunately, American ships were yet to see these shine from America's shores. Instead, Stephen Pleasonton's associate, Winslow Lewis, had developed in 1810 his own version of the Argand lamp and had sold the patent to the United States government just before the outbreak of the War of 1812. By 1815, all the lighthouses along the coast had a Lewis lamp. The lantern room at Cape Cod Light, for example, had 15 new lamps arranged in two circular, horizontal rows. The outer, lower row held eight of the Lewis lamps, and the inner, upper row held seven; however, none of these was aimed due south across the lower Cape lands of Eastham and Chatham and Monomoy. Together with 15 inch reflectors, though, the 15 new lamps were capable of sending out a brighter beam across the other 300 degrees of the compass.

While Lewis' invention required only half the oil of the old spider lamps, the Lewis lamp was simply not as intense as the Argand lamp then being used in Europe. One reason was the early attempts by Lewis to increase each lamp's intensity by placing a lens in front of the flame. The idea made some sense, because it was supposed to concentrate the straying beams of light. However, these lenses were removed before too long because they tended to block the beam instead.

The major reason, however, for the relative inferiority of the Lewis lamp was the shape of the so-called parabolic reflector. According to government reports, these tended to be less like reflecting mirrors and more like shaving basins. Their silver finish was too thin to withstand the daily cleaning, and their

Etching of Sands Point Light at western end of Long Island.

basic metal was unable to hold its parabolic shape. In fact, these reflectors were often reported to be more spherical than parabolic. By 1839, however, the Cape Cod Light had installed newer, 21 inch parabolic reflectors.

A lantern was more than just a light. The principles behind its form were not unlike those of a hand-held lantern; the scale was simply enlarged to the size of an entire room. At the top of every lighthouse, for example, a hole resembling the center of a funnel was made to allow the rising smoke and fumes from all the lamps in the lantern room to vent themselves into a flue between the ceiling and the cap. From there it could escape through trough-like gutters which then spilled down above the outside of the sashes. Just inside these sashes were a set of hooks on which a drape could hang across the plate glass windows of the lantern.

Every able keeper understood that the center of a flame must be exactly opposite the center of its reflector in order to be most efficient. As with every lens, however, whatever glass disperses the rays of light outward from one side must conversely concentrate them inward whenever light shines from the opposite direction. The reflectors served the same principles. To a careful keeper that all meant drawing the drape past his lantern room windows and turning down all his wicks in the morning. Otherwise the warm sunlight falling upon the reflectors would set them all afire, even on the coldest day.

This was the work of the poorer reflectors. Technically, the concentrated beam produced by a parabolic reflector was the result of something called the catoptric system. By 1820 the British had made refined reflectors out of silver-coated copper, which could take a single Argand lamp and make it shine with the light of nearly 3,000 candles.

Not long after that, yet another technological advancement had been made in France when Augustin Fresnel produced a lens that used the dioptric system. While the catoptric system of the parabolic reflector bounced the light into a stronger beam, the dioptric system of the Fresnel lens used a set of prisms to collect and bend and aim whatever light came from an Argand lamp. Eventually, these lenses and the light they produced would be categorized into orders, each determined by the distance from the light source itself to the lens.

Etching of Bird Island Light, Massachusetts.

Horton's Point Light is the the easternmost lighthouse on the North Fork of Long Island.

A so-called first order lens was both the largest and the brightest of the four most common sizes, and it measured 36.2 inches from light source to lens glass. A lens of the second order was 27.6 inches; of the third order, 19.7 inches; and the fourth, 9.8. The first two orders were used for seacoast lights, and the others were used more commonly for harbor and range lights.

The basic result of Fresnel's invention was the creation of the most efficient lantern yet, not simply one which lost no light beams to the ceiling or the floor, to the heavens or the ocean, but also one which saved more ships out on the seas. Using a single Argand lamp, the Fresnel lens could create a beam as bright as 80,000 candles, the equivalent of today's automobile headlight. With the Fresnel lens, moreover, that beam of light could be shone directly where the sailors needed it most.

Due to the close relationship between Lewis and Pleasonton, however, the Fresnel lens was slow in reaching the shores of America. For all the changes that were being made in shipbuilding and ship propulsion, as well as all the changes coming about in lighthouse tower construction, the light remained less than its brightest. In the years before the Civil War, the United States government had purchased three of these Fresnel lenses for experimentation, and one was placed out at Sankaty Head on Nantucket in 1851.

Meanwhile, though, the Lewis lamp continued to find friends in high places, and the installation of the Argand lamp would never take place on the coast of Cape Cod. Instead, the lighthouse would be equipped with yet another type of lamp which would better deliver the fuel directly to the flame. This was a blessing for the keeper, because the use of the Fresnel lens also meant the need for fewer lamps. The 15 Lewis lamps in Cape Cod Light, for example, were replaced with a single, four-wick hydraulic lamp. With these improvements, though, came a complicated set of cogs and springs and pumps which baffled any keeper who had lacked the necessary mechanical inclination.

These particular lamps would also be among the last to burn whale oil being brought back to these shores in dwindling quantities by the fleets from Nantucket and New Bedford. By 1860, the keeper of Cape Cod Light would be relying upon lard oil and eventually kerosene. That final switch in the 1880s to an oil which had been refined, rather than one which had been rendered, would help reduce the keeper's worry about New England's cold temperatures per-

The Indian Neck Lighthouse at Rockport, Maine, still maintains the dwelling whose style once characterized a good many of the stations along the New England coast.

vading the tower and congealing any animal oils into thickened lumps of fat. At the time of the installation of the hydraulic lamps, though, the winter oil still remained a problem, and so did the lamps themselves.

These hydraulic lamps, after all, represented the first real pieces of machinery in a New England lighthouse. Fog bells and steam whistles were sometimes employing clockworks and large engines, but these lamps were more complicated gadgets. Their function was to keep the level of the oil inside the wick just below the very burning of the flame, and they seemed both intricate and delicate. In the event there was any problem or question with these new contraptions, the keeper need only read the instructions. All too often up to this point, however, a keeper's qualifications might not have included that skill and

usually there was no one else around. Experience soon became a teacher at the risk of causing a shipwreck on the shore.

If the hydraulic lamps presented an occasional drawback, though, then at least the Fresnel lens provided a steady performance. More than either the catoptric system, or even the original dioptric system, today's Fresnel lens is called a catadioptric system, because it contains elements of both. Each lens panel in this particular system consists of a central bull's-eye lens which concentrates the rays that come horizontally from the lamp. Above and below each panel, the system holds a series of prisms; the lower rings refract the light up to the same beam as the bull's-eye lens, while the upper rings refract the light down to it. This results in a single, concentrated beam far more intense than any other to date.

Most often in lighthouses, these panels are formed into a cone-shaped lens which resembles a bee-hive standing nearly 12 feet tall. Then, if the Fresnel lens is rotated, the moving set of bull's-eye lenses present the effect of a flashing beacon. Unlike the eclipser, though, this beacon never loses its luminous range; it only grows in intensity as the bull's-eye passes between the lamp in the tower and the observer out at sea.

The Fresnel lens installed in Cape Cod Light was not the catadioptric system, but rather the original dioptric system. Lacking the bull's-eye lens in the middle panel, the lens instead was rectangular, but still a vast improvement over the Lewis version of the Argand lamp. This light would remain about the same until the turn of the century, when once again the government decided that the Cape Cod Light should flash.

By October of 1901 the lamp, which stood a full 12 feet tall and reached some 6 feet in diameter, was sitting upon a chariot and floating on a frictionless pool of liquid mercury that allowed the lamp to revolve with the least amount of effort. Through the deck of the lantern room to the watch room right below it, a massive clockwork system was hung to rotate the heavy lamp. Though somewhat cumbersome, the clockwork was not intricate.

Basically, it consisted of a large steel drum, around which was wrapped a weighted cord. By engaging a clutch, the keeper could turn a hand crank to wind the cord around the drum without moving the lamp. Then, as gravity

pulled the weight on the end of the cord straight down through the lantern room deck, the drum would turn and a set of gears would mesh with the cog wheel at the base of the lens chariot and rotate the Cape Cod Light. As it flashed once every four seconds, mariners needed only to refer to their light list to know which government lighthouse stood within their sight.

With the addition of the flashing signal at the High Lands came other 20th century advancements, which would begin to transform the basic function of the lighthouse out in Truro and along the coastline of the United States. By 1904, the government had established a United States Naval Radio Station on the lighthouse grounds and this, in turn, became a radio compass station. With the rapid development of the radio compass and the radio beacon, in time both would replace the need for most ships to visibly see any light upon New England's shore. This has become the fate of most of the lights throughout New England and the nation. While each lighthouse remains more than merely decorative, its visible beam stands to serve the less sophisticated sailors.

That has not meant the end to continued improved conditions in New England's lighthouses. Although an electric light was slow to come to the High Lands tower, come it did in 1931 when the last of the oil lamps was replaced with a 1,000 watt bulb inside the Fresnel lens. Actually, more than one was first placed inside on a starfish-looking mechanism which rotated automatically to a newer, working bulb whenever one burns out. Finally, in 1945 the Fresnel lens was dismantled and scrapped to make way for two pair of rotating beacons which together send out four beams of 4,000,000 candlepower each. Shaped more like drums, the lamps have a 36 inch lens on each end and are set one on top of the other so that the lamps are 180 degrees apart. The lenses now are circular, more like those in an airport tower, and behind each shines a 1,000 watt bulb. It is paired with another bulb set to rotate into place when the first bulb burns out. An electric motor drives the mechanism that continues to ro-

Originally upon Colchester Reef to warn captains away from one of the worst shipping hazards in Lake Champlain, this Vermont lighthouse has been carefully relocated and restored upon the grounds of the Shelburne Museum. Built in 1871, it is identical to the two Rhode Island stations constructed during the same period at Sabins Point and Pomham Rocks, as well as the stone variation built upon Connecticut's Penfield Reef.

tate the four beacons at the same rate of one flash every four seconds. Gone is the fabled flame, and with it the legendary keeper.

For lighthouse romantics it has become somewhat disparaging to accept the reality that a keeper's work has become little more than that of a handy man of sorts, changing light bulbs once a month and cleaning lenses even less. Of all the lighthouses which at one time or another have stood along New England's shores, Boston Light was the first to get its keeper simply because it was the first lighthouse to be built in this New World. Now, however, of all the lights remaining in America's service, only Boston Light stands the greatest chance of retaining an on-site keeper. All the others will have been automated, and with that some will have had their outbuildings demolished as well.

Clearly, then, a good part of the living romance will begin to vanish. No longer will the folks in town imagine how the keeper of the light is faring in a storm. No longer will the seamen on their bridges search the far horizon throughout the nights of starless darkness. And those along the shore who yearn to think that somewhere on the ocean stands a sailor on the watch will need to look beyond the lighthouse for some common point of focus.

Still, the legacy of the New England lighthouse keeper endures.

KEEPERS OF THE FLAME

For one thing, there were the keeper's duties, sometimes arduous, but seldom intellectual. Early generations of keepers tending spider lamps often needed only to fill the pans with oil, light the wicks, and clean the panes of glass quite often. Later generations tending to the Lewis version of the Argand lamp, had to trim the wicks, clean the chimneys, and avoid doing whatever might possibly scratch the parabolic reflectors. For this, they came to be known more affectionately as "wickies" and as long as the keeper was attentive each night, was fully prepared for the following night by the middle of each morning, and was tidy enough to apply to his cleaning the minimal efforts of a "Scotch lick" then the primary routine required little more than stamina and common sense.

But "keep" is a word that deserves more thought than most folks tend to give it. As innocent as it may look at first, the syllable resounds with trust, as well as obligation. Consider, for example, what a person did to lay claims to being a keeper. In general, one must keep alert, keep watch, keep calm, keep clean, keep accounts, keep at hand, keep house, keep track of time, and always try to keep healthy. Often, this was done, of course, to keep a ship away from harm, or else to keep some hope alive. After all, in keeping to themselves they had become dedicated keepers of faith, the faith that bonded keepers and captains together through the dangers of darkness. Such devotion generally ran deep, and often it revealed itself in manners most dramatic.

Legend, for example, tells how Keeper Fred Jordan at the Penfield Reef Lighthouse, just off Fairfield, Connecticut, was taking his holiday leave at the height of a winter storm on the eve of Christmas in 1916. While he attempted to row ashore that night, the pull on his oar provided no match for the billowing of the seas, and in one swift swell his craft capsized, sending him into the

During the Hurricane of 1938, storm tides not only ripped away the platform which encircled Saybrook Breakwater Light, but also washed away some of the granite blocks which made up the jetty itself.

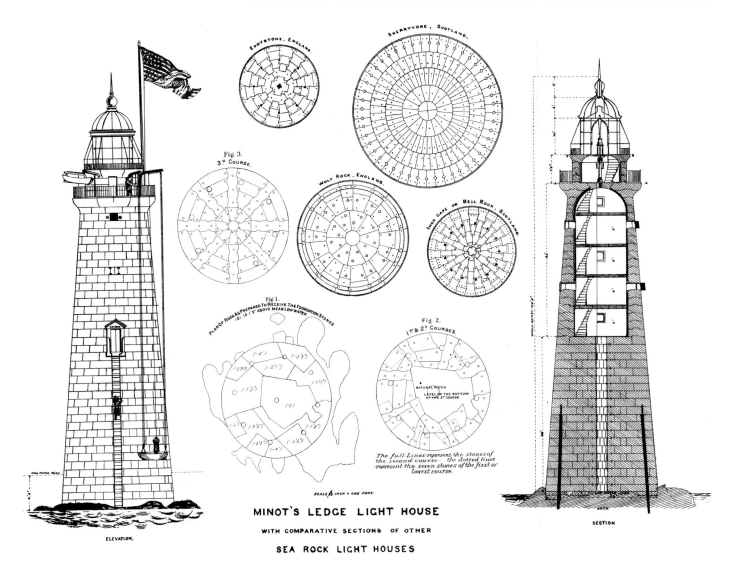

MINOT'S LEDGE LIGHT HOUSE

WITH COMPARATIVE SECTIONS OF OTHER

SEA ROCK LIGHT HOUSES

Etching of plans for Minots Ledge with diagrams of stone courses from other lights outside New England.

Sound. At least his body was recovered, and in the pocket of his coat was found a note that Jordan had written to Captain Iten, another Penfield keeper. Apparently, Jordan had forgotten to leave behind the message that Iten should complete the journal entries for December 24, 1916; however, Jordan knew that lighthouse records had to be kept up-to-date.

Those who came to replace Jordan have told of sights that some have since then seen. A shadowy figure has danced on the riprap; another has been seen in the storm deck above; and still others tell the story of a phantom in a row-boat who has piloted lost vessels to safety. The strangest sight of all, however, happened one night without any warning. A figure in white drifted forth from a room at the lighthouse, then floated down the staircase, only to vanish outside in the dark.

Those who followed him searched throughout the Penfield Reef Lighthouse station, and found that someone had been in the records room where all the old logs were still kept. On the table the journal of 1916 was open, and the page was turned to that of the fateful Christmas Eve when Keeper Jordan had drowned. Fortunately, Keeper Iten had kept the records up-to-date, just as the note had instructed. Time and time again, the legend still repeats the tale of how some spirit has been there to read the entry made by Keeper Iten, which told of the death of the keeper named Fred Jordan. Perhaps death was some-

thing the spirit found too trying to accept, especially when Keeper Jordan knew he had left his job unfinished. Devotion to a job could do that to a person, especially when his lot on earth might be confined to such a tiny little territory as the Penfield Reef.

"It requires a lot of philosophy to be a light-keeper on an outside station," remarked the late Captain Charles Hinckley, who had served five miles off Cape Cod in the lighthouse that marked the rocks known as Bishop & Clerks. Built in 1858, the granite tower was damaged by a storm in 1935, then demolished by the Coast Guard in 1952. Much like the structure at Minots Ledge, the tower at Bishop & Clerks emerged straight up from a ledge beneath the waters, so it served both as a dwelling and a light. "The trouble with our life here," remarked a keeper at Minots Ledge, "is that we have too much time to think."

That did not mean that there were an extraordinary number of idle hours in a keeper's day. On the contrary, there were many duties, most of which were mindless chores that could be handled while contemplating other matters. Aside from tending to the lantern at regular intervals throughout the hours of darkness, a keeper then had to refill the lamps and trim the wicks by 10 a.m. in preparation for the coming night. In addition, the brass and glass of the lantern room and tower required constant cleaning and polishing, as well as occasional replacement and repair. Beyond the tower itself, the entire station demanded

The Maritime shores of Peggy's Cove stand as evidence that the differences between the navigational hazards of Nova Scotia and the ones Down East in Maine are simply a matter of politics, not geology.

Reaching 137 feet above the surrounding sea, the beacon atop the Boon Island Lighthouse sits atop the tallest lighthouse tower in Maine. Situated eight miles off the coast of York, keepers in the past often communicated with the mainland by means of carrier pigeons.

As workers reshingle the dwelling at the lighthouse on Mt. Desert Rock, far across the Gulf of Maine looms Cadillac Mountain to the north. As a seamark along the entire Atlantic coastline, the mountain has no rival in the northern hemisphere.

the sort of constant attention that ranged from ordinary housekeeping and maintenance to bookkeeping and management.

Always there were other tasks that needed tending. If an outside station had any room for a boatshed and a landing, then a high wind or a heavy sea might inflict some damage demanding his attention. Inside and out, the tower needed constant care. The spiral staircase needed painting, as did the lantern's decks; walls had to be kept free of cracks, whose presence not only weakened the tower against the winds, but also made for cold conditions that threatened to thicken the oil; and always panes of glass had to be replaced. Sands driven by the winds would etch the surface and diminish the light, and now and then a bird or two would smash against the lantern panes. To neglect any one of these most commonplace occurrences would be to invite a complication at some inconvenient time. A conscientious keeper understood his responsibility.

That is why from the earliest of available openings at New England's lighthouse stations, the job of keeper seemed most fitting for any one of a number of folks whose interests had already taken them to sea. "We know how eyes may be strained in thick weather at sea to get hold of the light," explained one such gent, "and that makes us painfully anxious to keep it up to its full power, especially when frosts or sea-scud dims the lantern; for that is the very time when minutes count for hours on board ship."

The distinctive markings of Head Harbour Light on New Brunswick's Campobello Island are characteristic of many Maritime towers, which are often painted with black or red stripes to set them apart from a background of snow-covered shores.

Still, not every lighthouse station was set on some edge of the mainland, where a keeper might maintain a homestead in town. More than a few became outposts of civilization that were set astride a sometimes savage sea. If a keeper was fortunate, then he might have either an assistant or his family to help. Quite commonly, his appointed assistant was his wife, who could reside there, more often than not, with their children. As a result, an offspring's upbringing would be centered around both the sea and the tasks that were always at hand. Raised in such surroundings, certain sons and daughters knew nothing more than what is was to be a keeper; some even knew what that meant, for that became their second nature. Nevertheless, by the end of the 19th century, every such wife and offspring of a lighthouse keeper who might aspire to rise to a similar position in life would have to meet the keeper's qualifications set forth by the Lighthouse Board.

In an effort to reduce political patronage in the system, the board had restricted appointees to those persons between 18 and 50 who not only could read, write, and maintain a ledger, but also could master the skills and rigors of a lighthouse station. Sometimes that entailed carpentry; other times, mechanics; and on some occasions, dangerous rescues. What a keeper did not know, he was expected to be able to find in his station's collection of reference manuals that explained almost everything from lens cleaning to lantern repair to

machinery operations. For recreational reading, there was also a more casual collection of about 40 books kept in a portable bookshelf at every station. Every three months or so, these would be taken to another lighthouse and replaced with another collection by the station tender who brought provisions. All this was the system's concept of doing battle with a keeper's desolation.

Some outside station sites even offered keepers and their families just a little more space than Bishop & Clerks or Minots Ledge. Even such bleak foundations as Mount Desert Rock, Boon Island, and Saddleback Ledge have some dry ground around them, but often their keepers have had soil bagged on the mainland in the spring, then hauled out to the stations, where cracks and crevices could be filled up with some fertile earth. In gentler moments, these keepers and their families have cultivated gardens and nurtured flowers, all of which are subject to destruction. But by the end of each winter, virtually every speck of soil has been swept away by water or by winds. Keepers, close-knit with their families, set their sights on spring's new promise, and a youngster in those settings sensed some value in such things.

Gardening, however, was not the only lesson to be gleaned from whatever earth and sea surrounded the lighthouse. As would later be learned at Penfield Reef, death would become a lesson all too often. So, too, was it a painful one at Maine's Boon Island Lighthouse in the 1870s. As with the tale of Fred Jordan,

Set across the waters from Rhode Island's rolling, fertile farmlands, the Sandy Point Light on Prudence Island appears to be a site quite free from any dangers. The Hurricane of 1938 proved that not to be the case.

Etching of one form of steam-generated fog signal.

not all the facets of the yarn are necessarily facts; not even the names of the supposed couple, recently married, who left the mainland for their assignment, are known. After living a number of untold months in matrimonial bliss, the young groom and keeper fell quite ill and, just as quickly, died. Even if fate had not planned it so, the storytellers did, and they still claim that on the very night the keeper died a storm blew in to beat upon Boon Island.

Devoted to her dead husband, as well as to the job which he now left her, the young widow set about attending to the light. Climbing the tower and lighting the lamps, she then returned to stay beside the body of her husband. Throughout the night, she kept her vigils–night watch and deathwatch. But come the morning, the storm still roared, and nothing diminished her efforts.

The second night she set the lights, and then again the night that followed. Each time, she returned to her dead husband until she lost all track of time whatsoever. As long as the storm had continued to rattle Boon Island, the widow would tend the lamps. And when the storm finally lost all its powers, so too had the widow lost her own. Weak and weary and without much reason at all, she left the lantern dark above Boon Island on that first calm night since her husband's death. At last she found moments for mourning. When curious fishermen arrived on the following day to determine the loss of the light, they found the young widow clambering about the rock-strewn island with an air of distraction, distraught with the fate of her lover.

Such devotion to the light would become the touchstone of many careers in the lighthouse service, even after the Lighthouse Board was formally dissolved by Congress in 1910 and replaced by a civilian Bureau of Lighthouses at the same time. Clearly, the old organization relinquished a more reputable light-

The lens at Cape Elizabeth's eastern lantern helps create a beacon with the power of 4 million candles, the most powerful of such lights along New England's shore.

house system than the one it had inherited from the superintendency of the fifth auditor. And before administration of the system was given to the Coast Guard in 1939, even greater changes would come about.

None of these calculated improvements, however, could ever overshadow the dedication of its emerging breed of keepers and their families. Such people in the 20th century have been exemplified by Keeper George Gustavus at Sandy Point Lighthouse in Rhode Island, as well Keeper Arthur Small, who tended the Palmer Island Lighthouse at New Bedford Harbor in Massachusetts.

At 14, Small had fished with the fleets out of Gloucester and Maine before he had served in the Navy. After that, he had worked on Coast Guard ships until joining up with the Lighthouse Service for almost 20 years. His experiences with the seas clearly ran deep, and were reflected through the authenticity displayed in his skillfully painted maritime scenes.

"Whenever they say anything about a lighthouse keeper, they always act as if he were some kind of hero. We are not heroes," Small had once insisted. "Here I am on this island, perfectly safe, working and painting pictures, while you wander around in New Bedford, crossing streets with automobiles and trolley cars whizzing by, just missing you by a few feet. Why, you people take more chances in a week than I do in ten years."

In general, that might well have been true, for—set between the shorelines of New Bedford and Fairhaven—Palmer Island was not so remote a site as many others throughout New England, but neither was it any less of a challenge in the face of the storm which was about to strike on September 21, 1938. Likewise, not many miles away on the eastern side of Prudence Island in Narragansett Bay, stood Sandy Point Lighthouse almost by itself upon the sandy beach just offshore from Portsmouth, Rhode Island. A couple hundred feet to the west was the keeper's dwelling, which that day was occupied by the Gustavus family, two friends of theirs named Lynch, and the septuagenarian Martin Thompson, who had been the light's keeper for nearly 20 years.

Not too many miles further to the south and west of both New Bedford and Prudence Island, Keeper Sidney Gross was quite literally battening down his hatches at the Saybrook Breakwater Lighthouse, just where the Connecticut River empties into Long Island Sound. He noted in his log at 2 p.m., that "a light southeast breeze sprung up from a perfect calm." Already up in New Bedford, Keeper Small could sense that something sinister was stirring in the air, so he set about to secure his station and to store for the night an added ration of oil, as well as additional lamps and wicks.

By 3 p.m. the breeze had blown into a gale. "I made several attempts to get outside to save some of the small articles on the platform, part of them not being lashed down," wrote Keeper Gross in Connecticut, "but I found it impossible, as the wind pushed me right back into the engine room." In Rhode Island, Thompson suggested that the keeper's dwelling was probably the safest place to be on Sandy Point, so he accompanied the Lynches, as well as the wife and son of Keeper Gustavus, to the upper floor of the quarters, while Gustavus himself stayed behind.

When the storm did strike, it would sweep across New Bedford Harbor with a wicked vengeance unlike that of any other gale ever witnessed by those then alive. This wind would prove to be no gale, however. It was an unforeseen hurricane, and seas grew restless in places such as Long Island Sound, Block Island Sound, and in Vineyard Sound as well.

Into New Bedford Harbor waves of water rolled, and the surge was engulfing the island. Even with the astronomical high tide still hours away, combers raced across the surface, and Keeper Small entreated his reluctant wife, Mabel, to join him in the lighthouse tower. However, she preferred to stay inside their dwelling. Not one to waste a moment's more time, the keeper hoisted her into his arms, then carried his wife to the shelter against her better wishes.

"At 6:00 pm the water was pouring through the second story window in the hall. I boarded up the window with the doors of a small cabinet and what loose material I could find," noted Gross, the keeper at Saybrook Breakwater. "Everything outside the building was now carried away, and I certainly did not expect to see another sunrise as the whole structure was shaking under the violent pounding."

Right up Narragansett, the storm surge swept, destroying whatever stood in its path and proving Thompson dead wrong. As the tidal wave shouldered its way past survivors, it carried every remnant of shelter as well. The wife and son of the keeper were last seen drifting away from safety, but the old man and the couple had already disappeared. Only Keeper Gustavus survived.

Meanwhile, due to pass by the Palmer Island Light at any moment was the

Aside from an inspector's claim made in 1842 that the lighthouse at Maine's Saddleback Ledge was the only one in New England designed by "an architect and engineer," this isolated station south of Isle au Haut Bay also has retained its notoriety for being the only one along the entire East Coast where a landing required a hoist and boom. Even on the calmest days, no tender can safely make a direct approach upon its rocks.

New Bedford boat from Nantucket, and Keeper Small was concerned that the fog signal should be sounding. Still, Mabel Small was not too happy, and while her husband tinkered with the signal, she darted back outside and headed for their house. Though he had seen her run away, he knew he could not stop her, and more than once along the way the waves had knocked her over. Finally, she found herself at the door of their home.

The tower, however, was still more secure, and Keeper Small knew that Mabel should be there. So, once he had started the fog signal's engine, he again set out for the dwelling. As his wife had before him, he had a tough time with the waves. A very tough time, indeed. One knocked the keeper's legs from beneath him, then sucked him into its undertow. Fighting against the current, Keeper Small was swimming beneath the water's surface until he at last found solid land.

All the while, Mabel was learning what her husband had feared—parts of their house were already gone, the walls had crumbled and ceilings were down. When Keeper Small finally caught up with his wife, she was sitting alone in a fog of her own. This time she wanted to go wherever he felt might be best. Yet, the only way to the tower was churning with the wind-whipped water.

Instead, the keeper and his wife headed for the higher ground of the oil shed. In one calculated moment, they dashed between the combers to the shed. Once inside, Keeper Small quickly ripped some shelving down, then braced the boards between some higher beams. Boosting his wife, he helped her climb upon them, high above the floor. That much done, the keeper was not certain he could hear the fog signal above the wind. He felt that if he could not hear it, then neither could the boat from Nantucket. So, he stepped outside the oil shed, leaned his body toward the wind, and headed for the tower.

Unbeknownst to Small, the Nantucket boat already had found a safer haven. Also unknown to him was the danger building not so far offshore. Just as the howl of the wind had hidden the sound of the signal, so too did it hide the oncoming rush of the waves, especially the mountainous one that swelled into New Bedford Harbor and measured close to 40 feet high. When the wave hit Palmer Island, it struck full force at the keeper as well and pulled him underwater again for the second time that day. This time Small was not the only flotsam bobbing and dipping and swirling through the harbor. From beaches and boatdecks and breakwaters along New Bedford and Fairhaven, the storm was collecting all sorts of debris, including the body of Lightkeeper Small. Still, he was alive and fairly aware, noticing at one time that the oil shed remained standing. He assumed that meant that his wife was still safe.

If fact, Mabel had witnessed her husband adrift in the turmoil, and she waded through the water to the boathouse. In winds surpassing 100 miles an hour, she tried to launch the lighthouse dory in hopes of rowing out to save the keeper. Mabel knew fully that her husband would have done the same; no doubt, she felt that they must live together or die the same. Perhaps it was fortunate then that Mabel was unaware of another surge about to hit the island. To think that such a wave might soon be separating her forever from her husband would probably have frightened her more than any other danger. She never saw the wave that took away the boathouse and the dory and their dwelling.

"I saw the great wave crash into the boathouse," Small later recounted. "It was the last thing I remember, for then I must have been hit by a big piece of timber and knocked unconscious."

It also was the last time he saw Mabel alive, two days before her 48th birthday. Trying to rescue her troubled husband, she had died in that crashing surf. Meanwhile in a state of shock, Keeper Small still kept the Palmer Island lamp alight throughout the raging storm and kept the signal sounding, too.

"When daylight came at last," wrote Gross at Saybrook, "what we saw seemed more like a dream than reality. There was nothing around the tower except the battery house, and even that was badly out of shape."

As was also the case at Sandy Point, at Palmer Island only the tower remained on the lighthouse station, and Small had kept to his post. Even when he was rescued the following morning, the Lighthouse Service was first contacted to grant permission for his departure from the station. "No keeper may leave his post until relieved, if he is able to walk," was the hard and fast rule.

Men such as Arthur Small were always aware that a keeper's foremost task was to keep his lamp lighted and help keep a ship from harm's way. Though their title was that of "lighthouse keeper" and not at all "lifesaver" these were the very people who soon became—if not the only people on the scene—most certainly the very first ones there. So it came in time to pass that handy men were more renowned as heroes.

HEROES OF THE COASTLINE

Throughout those early years, there were countless times when a well-maintained lighthouse lantern was simply not enough. No solid tower ranging high above New England's shore, no well-trimmed lamp shining brightly through a lantern's pane, no alarming noise from a bell or a horn might ever pierce through walls of certain conditions that persist along this coast. Solid sheets of swirling snow, or close-knit blankets of fog could shatter and stop any erstwhile beam of light, just as they might disorient the world's most skillful master studying his compass. Whistles and cannon and trumpets and bells could be drowned by the pound of relentless surf, or the howl of a furious wind through the lines above a deck. During such times evidence soon became the only thing that might ever stand out in the clear. A lighthouse could not save a crew trapped in peril. Only a keeper could.

Without a keeper, the lighthouse was little more than another building, no different from the oil shed or the boathouse or even the keeper's dwelling. If that lighthouse should ever fail to function, a keeper could only resort to basic human nature, namely, the instinct to survive. This meant the survival of other lives at the risk of the keepers' losing their own. These keepers and their families were special folks indeed, ones who felt a calling for their work not unlike those who joined the clergy.

"Of course, it's terrible lonesome, especially in dirty weather, but we're used to lonesomeness," admitted one keeper of a light along the coast of Maine whose two children had been overwhelmed by the rush of a sudden tide. Their son and daughter, ages 10 and 12, had been exploring the rocks at the edge of their father's station when both of them were caught unawares and drowned. Still, their parents remained at the post Down East.

The granite for the tower of Petit Manan Light was first cut and assembled in Trenton, Maine, where the pieces were numbered, disassembled, then shipped to the island site. There the pieces were again put together in 1817 to create a tower that stands 127 feet tall.

In 1890, the cast-iron tower of Eastern Point Lighthouse replaced the one at Gloucester Harbor that had first been built in 1832. Lobsters thrive in these rocky shores and cold waters north of Boston, which are more like those of Maine than the sandy beaches of Massachusetts further south.

"Someone has to keep this light," the keeper explained, "and my wife and I think it's just our job in life. No one much knows about us away off here, but we know we're doing something important. If we were on the mainland, we'd just be looking out for ourselves the way most mainland folks do. We always wanted everything best for our children; and now we know they're getting better things than we could have given them. Maybe that would sound foolish to some folks, but when you're way out here with only God and what He's made for real steady company, you get to believing in Him and in what He has planned for us all. If my wife wanted to leave I'd go, too, of course; but she wants to stay the same as I do."

That one particular story befits another of the keeper at Hendrick's Head Light, two miles up the Sheepscot River in Maine, long before the station was automated in 1975. A century earlier, a square wooden tower—quite like the one built the same year out on the Provincetown sands of Long Point at the very tip of Cape Cod—was constructed on the rocks atop Hendrick's Head to replace the original structure of 1829. Just about that time, the keeper was reminded all too forcefully of the frustrating limitations which the New England weather could impose upon his light.

Among every keeper's greatest fears is that at some especially crucial time the station could fail to provide any guidance at all. Quite sadly at first, this

keeper's fears were realized when a schooner sailing blindly through the snow on the Sheepscot River "fetched up all standing" on a ledge only a half a mile from the lighthouse, which finally became visible too late at Hendrick's Head.

Barely conspicuous from the lighthouse, passengers and crew alike clung fast to whatever lines and rigging they might reach, and climbed as high as they could above the deck, for though the vessel was well upriver, the seas of this storm were heavy and cold. Sometimes rising to heights of 10 feet, and other times close to 15, wave upon wave continued to crest without pity right over the ship, and often flung higher their wind-driven sprays that froze to the canvas and clothing. From moment to moment, these people were trying their best to survive, drenched by the surf, whipped by the blizzard, and literally freezing in place.

Onshore the surf was surely no less violent, and the keeper was flustered in his attempts to launch his rowboat into the frenzied Sheepscot. Desperate and dismayed, he abandoned almost every expectation that his dory might ever reach those frozen few offshore. Still, the keeper and his wife set ablaze on the riverbank the largest of fires that the storm would allow. Save for that flames and the ones that flickered more steadily from the lighthouse lantern above, the shades of dusk pushed their frigid ways between the flakes of falling snow. Through the blackness that covered the rigging, some figures still held on for life, whiles others simply did their best to shape any hold at all. Alive or dead, their ordeal was not one that passed unnoticed. Time and again the keeper ventured near the rocky ledge and hoped against hope that he might do more.

On one such foray, the keeper stared hard into the storm as his eyes could discern some approaching wreckage rising and falling in the seas that washed toward the shore. With both a boat hook and a piece of line in hand, he marked time on the rocks along the Sheepscot until he was almost certain where this flotsam might come ashore. Almost without patience he waited as it drifted toward a nearby cove, then bobbed its way past the closer shoreline. If nothing less, the wreckage provided some moments of intense concentration as the storm still vented its wrath all around.

Then, unable to wait any longer, the keeper lashed the line around his waist and ordered his wife to tether the other end somewhere off in the darkness. Into the water went the keeper, a salvor obsessed with the thought that something of this ship should be saved. Beaten back by a breaker, he struggled forward one more time until he had managed to hook up the wreckage. Then he grabbed hold of the object and dragged it as best he could, before he might be forced to ride it astride some foaming crest of the waves that were beating their waters toward the shore.

In the calmer turmoil of the storm on land, the keeper then realized that his efforts had gone into salvaging a feather bed. Not simply a feather bed, though, it was actually two of them deliberately bound up taut to serve quite possibly some other purpose. The keeper then decided to cut the bonds and found a box inside. Safe within that, a restless baby girl lay shrieking and full of life! Together, the keeper, his wife, and this newfound child all made their way back to the warmth and safety of their dwelling.

As the keeper's wife provided comfort, the keeper once again went out, this time to somehow signal to those still on board that this small child was safe and sound. Beyond the light of the fire and deep within the swirling squall, the fated vessel somewhere wallowed, now altogether out of sight of land. No one not even a solitary, stiffened sailor—could be made out in the darkness there. Very soon, however, other debris could be seen, and ominous bits and pieces washed ashore.

Perhaps disheartened once and for all, the keeper retrieved the remaining bits of the wreckage that had come ashore with the babe. This included the baby's blankets, a locket, and the mother's message written in hopes of commending her child unto God. Her daughter, however, had not died. Instead, she had drifted into the arms of a keeper and his wife who had not long before given a child of their own up to Heaven. And so, on an otherwise desperate night for a dedicated keeper, a baby girl had brought a light of her own to the life of two other souls. Legally adopted by the couple who saved her, she was raised as a lighthouse child.

Not every such storm that might batter New England, however, could make of a lighthouse keeper a hero, and even those storms which were met with such deeds quite often provided sad endings. Already that had happened just a generation earlier in the shoal-infested waters that plague Ipswich, north of Boston. Three great hurricanes had swept New England back in 1839, and two days before Christmas the second of those storms had caught the schooner *Deposit* unaware on her passage out of Belfast, Maine.

Built only two years earlier, the Ipswich Light at Crane's Beach, just south of Newburyport's Plum Island, was actually a range light that guided ships into the channel at Ipswich Harbor. The station consisted of two square towers, set carefully together—as all range lights are—to indicate to any pilot that his ship was sailing mid-channel whenever he aligned the beacon in front with the other one not too far to the rear. Before they were finally dismantled, the two Ipswich towers had been moved nine times to account for the shifts in the harbor channel.

Aboard the *Deposit* on December 23, 1839 was Captain Cotterell, and at the Ipswich Lighthouse, Keeper T.S. Greenwood. Unfortunately, though, neither one had seen the other until the ship had run aground. At daybreak, a townsman named Marshall could see the *Deposit* beached on the shoals, where she had been foundering for hours since midnight. By then, all hands had taken to the rigging, and passengers had joined them there. The winter winds had beaten throughout the dark of night, while breakers—too rampant for any sort of lifeboat to ever be able to stand much of a chance—had tortured the hull close to splintering. Captain Cotterell's wife had held her own among the others, but two of his seamen had succumbed to the pommeling, which was as taxing to the emotions as it could be to the body.

Keeper Greenwood arrived with Marshall, but neither one could foresee any moment when their lifeboat might ever get off from the shore. The surf seemed insurmountable. Then, however, the wailing wife of Captain Cotterell was heard from the rigging of the *Deposit*, and it was a poignant plea that could not be ignored.

As good a swimmer as he was, the keeper understood the danger of the storm, not too mention the overpowering strength of the undertow that lurked along that shoreline. Still, he answered the call of the captain's wife by

tying a line to his waist and entrusting the rest of the coil to Marshall with these orders: hold fast to the line until I am aboard the battered schooner, then secure this end to the lighthouse dory. The wind and the waves were much worse than expected; however, Keeper Greenwood had performed his first miracle of sorts. Weary from his struggling swim, he fought his way further through the foam that engulfed the *Deposit*, then he struggled to pull himself up to the bowsprit. Once there, he tied his end of the 200 foot line around the rigging, and waved for Marshall to shove out the boat. The man onshore hesitated, waiting once more for the opportune moment.

Suddenly it struck, and Marshall launched the lighthouse dory, at the same time jumping snugly toward its floorboards. Rising and falling, sliding and dipping, the dory was tugged through the surge by the keeper. Slowly it moved, sometimes taking on water from the bow, while other times taking on water past the gunwales. Finally, Marshall's dory reached the *Deposit*, and another minor miracle was performed.

Keeper Greenwood took command and first helped the wearied captain toward the bouncing dory. With his body beyond the point of aching numbness and his mind approaching unconsciousness, Cotterell stepped into the smaller vessel. However, both the captain and the keeper's helper were overtaken by the seas, which swept them underwater with the dory. From the schooner, the

Unlike the stations in Maine which stand upon more solid ground, Cape Cod Light shares a similar situation with those at Nauset and Chatham, as well as at Sankaty Head on the island of Nantucket. Every Atlantic wave that breaches upon their beaches below carries out to the sea some part of the shore.

Sitting at the easternmost point of the United States, the red and white striped lighthouse at West Quoddy Head overlooks Quoddy Narrows, the dramatic tides in the Bay of Fundy and Campobello Island.

Etching of Sankaty Head Light, Nantucket.

Etching of Sankaty Head Light, Nantucket.

keeper lowered a lifeline, but the only hand that had grabbed it was Marshall's. No one could see the captain, and no one would see him alive evermore. The lifeboat, too, was gone for good, and the episode then proved to be far too much for the captain's wife, now a widow, and the woman wailed out her grief.

Nothing might ever prepare any keeper for such an unlikely predicament. Still, Greenwood did his best to improvise as the storm showed some signs of subsiding. As the seas became less violent, the only two surviving members of the crew succeeded in drifting ashore upon wreckage. Meanwhile, the keeper and Marshall helped console the captain's distraught widow, then coaxed her to jump to the water with them. Finally, she agreed. Off the stern, the three of them plunged, where they discovered that they could touch bottom and still keep their heads above water. Regaining some composure there, the widow and her rescuers all floated together to the safety of shore.

The ordeal of winter winds and waters had seemed to be the worst that one might ever suffer along New England's coast, and yet there came another tribulation possibly more severe. This one transpired over several hours in January of 1885 just off the Cape Elizabeth Light, south of Portland, Maine.

As Ipswich Light, Cape Elizabeth Light consisted of two towers; however, these were no harbor range lights. On the contrary, this station provided in its easternmost tower a seacoast beacon whose powers would rival those other great lamps at Cape Cod and Sankaty Head. Though even the fifth auditor himself had questioned the necessity of having two lights at this station, the two brownish, rubble towers were commissioned in 1828, then painted years later with red markings in 1865 to distinguish them further in daylight. The west tower boasted a broad, vertical stripe; the east, four horizontal bands. By 1870, another outbuilding was added to the station to house the steam plant for a 10 inch locomotive whistle that might blast through the coastal fog for eight seconds of every minute.

Then Keeper Marcus Hanna arrived, and even more changes took place. The old towers were replaced with cast iron ones, and the lamps were made even more distinguishable than simply standing some 900 feet apart. One light remained fixed, while the other became flashing. Finally, the locomotive whistle was replaced by a siren, and everything seemed more than adequate. Nonetheless, by 1885 the nature of New England finally rose to meet the challenge that had been implied by the improvements at Cape Elizabeth.

In the early evening hours of that January night, Captain J.W. Lewis sailed his schooner, the *Australia*, from the harbor down at Boothbay with the aid of his two-man crew. Bound for Boston on an evening breeze, Lewis had on board only Austin Kellar and Irving Pierce, a cargo of ice from the Kennebec stored in her hold, and some barrels of mackerel lashed to the deck. By midnight, the storm had become a full-blown gale with temperatures down close to zero. When the *Australia* had come near the light at Halfway Rock, located between those at Seguin and Portland Head, the captain decided to steer her to Portland; however, visibility was nil.

So severe, in fact, were conditions that at Cape Elizabeth Keeper Hanna met up with frustration. Already weakened by a taxing cold, Hanna had become dispirited as well, for he knew that no master alert on a deck could be warned by his light or his siren. The winds at that speed simply shrieked through the shrouds, masking any such sound on the seas. Captain Lewis, however, was quite certain that he heard the keeper's signal, and he set his course to follow it toward port. Unfortunately, the sound that he heard had been coming from the Boston steamer, and the *Australia* soon lost all her bearings.

Before dawn, Hanna knew well that his spirit was willing, but his body was weak. Fortunately, Hiram Staples, the assistant keeper, relieved him of his post at 6 a.m. Even then, Keeper Hanna quite literally crawled home through the drifts that made his dwelling seem further away. There his wife put him to bed and said she would tend to the light come the daybreak.

By then, Captain Lewis and his crew had finally caught the sound of the siren, and in the dark before the dawn the captain decided to run the *Australia* straight ahead toward the station that they still could not see. Even if she went aground, he thought, at least there might be some greater chance of rescue. Soon he would find out. The *Australia* ran upon Dyers Ledge, and the three men all took to the rigging.

As had happened to the *Deposit* off Ipswich, this ship and its people became laden with ice. Already, they had jettisoned as much as possible of the *Australia's* cargo in hopes of keeping the vessel afloat. Even so, the weight of the ship became greater with the frozen spray, as did the weight of their clothes. Frozen in place above the decks, not one of them could move on his own. Only the winds and the waters might budge them now, much as one mountainous wave then knocked the captain from his perch. Struggling up from the boards, Lewis once more clambered for some safety, however momentary. Not long after, though, another wave swept him to the sea.

Staples had never caught sight the wreck, even though it sat just off his station. Instead, the keeper's wife had suddenly come upon the disaster as she worked her way from the tower. Mrs. Hanna roused her husband from his sickbed, and he then summoned Staples. With a coil of line and a weight for throwing, the men both hastened to the foundering schooner.

Unable to move at all by now, both Kellar and Pierce saw the two men from the lighthouse station work their way across the rocks, covered with layer upon layer of salty spray that had turned to ice through the night. Slowly, the men on the land inched their way closer down into the sea, and then they tried launching the line. With the weight on one end and the wind off the water, the rope never stood any chance. On each attempt it fell into the waves; on each retrieval it stayed stiff. Almost blinded from exposure, the seamen saw no signs of hope, especially when Staples and Hanna together had seemed to abandon their efforts on the shore.

The keepers of Cape Elizabeth's Light were working the feeling back into their bodies in the warmth of the inside shelter, however, and Hanna had every intention of trying once more to save both the crewmen outside. He simply was waiting for strength to return to his limbs when a deafening roar struck the schooner on the ledge. In the wake of such thunder, no flash ever follows. There's only the flood of more water. This time, however, such an adversity had suddenly turned to advantage. The vessel had been knocked fully clear of the ledge and pushed hard toward the rocks on the shore.

Marcus Hanna moved as quickly as his legs and the storm would allow, and he found the *Australia* nearby. Still frozen, the line he threw this time fell onto the ship; however, neither Kellar, nor Pierce could move to fetch it, and it soon washed away overboard. Undaunted, Keeper Hanna pushed into the sea again to retrieve the line and heave it one more time. Meanwhile, Pierce struggled his way free and readied himself for the effort. Finally, but ever so slowly, he managed to grasp hold of the icy line, then wrap the frozen cable around his waist.

Joyously, Hanna yelled for help, for he knew he could never bring the man ashore alone. But no one heard his plea. With anxiety at its height on both ends of the line, Pierce waited for the right moment, then slid into the sea. With uncertain footing, the keeper summoned whatever strength remained and tried to haul the seaman onto shore. Already Pierce was heavy with icy clothing, and the line itself allowed no supple slack. Nevertheless, the keeper made painstaking progress, hand over aching hand, while the helpless sailor bobbed through crests and troughs. When at last the battered body was in reach, Hanna doubted that he had the strength to bring what the keeper called this "frozen lump of humanity" up out of the water. Yet, the keeper somehow succeeded.

Except for the frozen form of Pierce collapsed upon the shore, Hanna still remained alone in facing the prospect of saving Kellar. Buoyed by his success, but sobered by his slackened strength, the keeper again tried to toss out his line, which sometimes was knocked from its course by the wreckage adrift in the water. At last, it fell within Kellar's feeble grasp, and the crewman found enough strength to wind it around him. Kellar let Hanna know when he was ready; however, Hanna knew that he himself was not. The sickness, the storm, and this prolonged struggle had all but sapped the keeper's last bit of strength. With a silent prayer, he signalled the sailor to take the plunge.

To his grateful surprise, Hanna was suddenly joined not only by Staples, but also by neighbors whom his wife had enlisted. Fresher arms and stronger backs pulled Kellar from the sea, then carried both of the sailors to shelter. Safe inside, the sailors finally found the strength to tell their tale in full, especially the fate of their captain. Marcus A. Hanna had saved the crew, but the body of Lewis would wash up on shore. Despite the fact that the keeper had bravely saved two lives, his lighthouse had failed for one other.

The octagonal tower that stands almost a hundred feet above New Haven's Five Mile Point is the station's second tower, built in 1847 of Connecticut sandstone and brick. Visible several hundred yards into the harbor's main channel is the Southwest Ledge, which replaced the beacon at Five Mile Point in 1877.

WOMEN OF VALOR

On June 11, 1833, Keeper Phineas Spear filled his time by measuring the dimensions of the granite pile which comprised Matinicus Rock, 22 miles off the New England coast where the imagined edge of Penobscot Bay washes into the Gulf of Maine. From end to end, the bleak, wave-swept surface was 2,350 feet long; from side to side, but 567 feet. He calculated this precisely to be 34.6 acres. Were this fertile farmland, it would have made sense for the keeper to total the island's surface in such terms; however, fertile farmland this was not.

This was Matinicus Rock, six miles distant from the tillable soil at the settlement on Matinicus Island. And measure it as he might, the keeper could never ignore the fact that his station was nothing much more than rock. The rock was one reason it was a hazard; the wind, the water, and the weather were the others. All told, these conditions were in need of a lighthouse, and twin wooden towers set astride a stone dwelling were placed on this edge in 1827.

Whipped by the wide-open winds of the winter and washed with the waves swelling white with their wrath, the towers could not tolerate that beating. Their first keeper, John Shaw, and his wife soon were pleading for more stable structures on Matinicus Rock. Keeper Thomas McKellar and his faithful family fled the light before the seas that surged up from the storm in January of 1839 tore the towers down upon the rocks. Darkness fell around the seas as well. Though mast-supported lamps were set out there to shed some light, not until 1846 were more rugged towers built, again at separate ends of a granite dwelling. By then, the Keeper Shaw had died, and so had Keeper Spear. After Shaw had first arrived, as many as six more keepers had come to stand watch, every moment well aware of the possibly that on any night the lighthouse might just surge off with the surf. Then came Keeper Samuel Burgess in 1853.

The clean, simple lines of the Maine's Fort Point Light in Searsport are the same as the lighthouse on Grindel Point across Penobscot Bay.

At the entrance to Cutler Harbor, Little River Light welcomes mariners into the shelter of this typically picturesque Maine haven.

Located on Mistake Island, Moose Peak Light guides the way into Jonesport, Maine, some five miles or more in the distance.

With him arrived his sickly wife, as well as their five children, a son and four daughters. Before long, the only son turned to fishing with a fleet in the Bay Chaleur, Down East in the Maritimes. That left with Burgess the oldest daughter of 14 years to help him tend to duties and to help his fragile wife bring up three others. So able would Abbie Burgess soon become that her father would look upon this daughter as his equal in their task. Wisely, she suggested late in 1855 that her mother's chambers be moved to another room behind the higher of the towers. Weeks later, a December storm proved that to have been a prudent decision. Then, in January, when Burgess was forced by short supplies to sail to Rockland for provisions, he left his daughter in charge of the lighthouse that stood on Matinicus Rock.

In his dory, Burgess set out for the mainland and, after he left, a nor'easter showed signs of approaching. For all intents and purposes, Abbie was now the household's head, and—at 16—the lighthouse keeper. So, through the night she trimmed the lamps that shone in both the towers, and in the morning she could see that the storm had not diminished. In fact, the nor'easter continued to blow even stronger, day after day, for three days more. Then came what little light the sky would allow through winter's fiercest furor.

"The new dwelling," Abbie later wrote in her personal journal, "was flooded

and the windows had to be secured to prevent the violence of the spray from breaking them in. As the tide came, the sea rose higher and higher, till the only endurable places were the light towers. If they stood, we were saved, otherwise our fate was only too certain. But for some reason, I know not why, I had no misgivings, and went on with my work as usual.

"For four weeks, owing to rough weather, no landing could be effected on the Rock. During this time we were without the assistance of any male member of our family," she added. "Though at times greatly exhausted with my labors, not once did the lights fail. Under God I was able to perform all my accustomed duties as well as my father's.

"You know," she continued in great detail, "the hens were our only companions. Becoming convinced, as the gale increased, that unless they were brought into the house they would be lost, I said to mother: 'I must try to save them.' She advised me not to attempt it. The thought, however, of parting with them without an effort was not to be endured, so seizing a basket, I ran out a few yards after the rollers had passed and the sea fell off a little, with the water knee deep, to the coop, and rescued all but one.

"It was the work of a moment, and I was back in the house with the door fastened, but I was none too quick, for at that instant my little sister, standing at the window, exclaimed: 'Oh, look! Look there! The worst sea is coming!'

"That wave destroyed the old dwelling and swept the Rock," she went on. "The sea is never still, and when agitated, its roar shuts out every other sound, even drowning our voices."

Abbie was more than competent, she was as dedicated and able as any other keeper. In some cases, no doubt, more so. Even after Abraham Lincoln later fired her father in 1861, Abbie Burgess remained on the Rock to assist the new keeper, John Grant, whose son she eventually married. Together, the younger Grants became parents of four children before they moved on to a lighthouse of their own, Down East at Whitehead Island.

Despite the near-legendary status of Abbie Burgess, her loyalty and stamina were neither greater, nor lesser than many other women, who—sometimes by design and often by chance—were thrust to the foreground of danger and given responsible roles. Perhaps the most recounted tales of such belong to the life of Newport's Ida Lewis, daughter of Captain Hosea Lewis, the first keeper at Rhode Island's Lime Rock Light.

Appointed to his post in 1854, when there was no dwelling at the lighthouse that could accommodate his family, Captain Lewis was the former pilot aboard a revenue cutter before he retired to a keeper's job when his health began to slip. A widower, he married a second time, and his new wife gave birth at their Newport house in 1842 to a girl, Idawalley. Though it well might seem an unusual name, Ida was never bothered by it. Too enthralled, perhaps, was she with the waters surrounding Aquidneck Island, the jut of Rhode Island territory that ran north and south to separate Narragansett from Mount Hope Bay.

Before the onset of her teenage years, young Ida excelled in both rowing and swimming. So, if she was excited when her father's appointment to Lime Rock Light took effect when she was 12, then it would be safe to state that she was most likely quite ecstatic when he had built for them there a large enough dwelling for his family to join him when she was 14. That was in June of 1858.

Displaying the sleek, rounded lines of art deco design, complete with skylights of glass blocks, the Cleveland Ledge Light is set upon a cast-iron caisson foundation in Buzzards Bay off Cape Cod.

By October of that very same year, Hosea Lewis had suffered a shock that restricted his actions much more. The elder Idawalley Lewis helped her husband tend the light, while the younger one tended the chores, including the ferrying by rowboat of her brothers and sister to the mainland schoolhouse each day.

"Old sailor that I am, I felt I would not give a penny for their lives," remarked the invalid captain upon observing their transport through some of New England's dirtiest weather. "I have watched them until I could bear it no longer, expecting at every moment to see them swamped and the crew at the mercy of the waves, and then I have turned away and said to my wife, 'Let me know if they get safe in,' for I could not endure to see them perish and realize that we were powerless to save them. You cannot tell the relief when she cried out, 'They have got safe to the rock, Father'."

At the age of 16, Ida made her first rescue, saving four wealthy youngsters who had endangered themselves with their roughhousing while sailing between the lighthouse and Fort Adams. At 24, she accomplished a similar feat in attempting to rescue three young, drunken veterans of the Civil War who had stolen her brother's boat. Two disappeared before she could arrive and were never heard from again, but the third soldier Ida managed to pull from the water and row to shore. In doing so, she strained herself with a severity that lasted for nearly a year.

One of her brothers claimed that she was able to "hold a boat to wind'ard in a gale better than any man I ever saw wet an oar. Yes," he went on, "and do it, too, when the sea is breaking over her."

Before 1869 was even halfway through, Ida had single-handedly rescued 11 grateful victims. Her reputation had become so widespread that the editor of *Harper's Weekly Magazine* wrote in June of that year that Ida was "likely to be more famous next summer than any Newport belle." The Life Saving Benevolent Society of New York had presented her with a silver medal plus an award of $100; the townsfolk of Newport recognized her efforts on the Fourth of July—proclaimed "Ida Lewis Day"—with the *Rescue*, her own lifeboat custom made by one of the finest local boat builders. President Grant came to visit with her at the Lime Rock Lighthouse that same year, as did the vice president, Schuyler Colfax.

In years to come, Ida would be honored by the Narragansett Boat Club, the prominent women's organization known as the Sorosis Society, the Rhode Island General Assembly, and the American Life Saving Society, which gave her yet another silver medal. Then, after her father finally died, Ida was named official keeper of Lime Rock Light following a special act of Congress in 1879. She was not the first woman keeper, for many wives and daughters had succeeded their husbands and fathers in similar posts. However, she kept watch over what some were then calling "the most faithfully tended light on the coast."

For more than half a century, she kept throughout the night the beacon which shined from the three-sided lantern in the tower at the southwest corner of their dwelling. "The light is my child," she had once said, "and I know when it needs me, even if I sleep." During the day, Ida kept watch toward the water, where she made her last rescue at the age of 64.

In all, Ida had saved, by some accounts, nearly 30 people from Rhode Island waters. The U.S. government awarded her a medal for "extreme heroic daring involving imminent personal danger," and the Massachusetts Humane Society presented the Rhode Islander with a silver medal for crawling across the frozen harbor to save two more soldiers from nearby Fort Adams. The troops presented her with a silver teapot.

By 1911, there was talk of closing down Lime Rock Light in favor of a newer station not far away on Goat Island. Some say the rumor devastated Ida, who was found unconscious from an apoplexy on the floor of the lighthouse early one October morning. Within three days she had died. As she had always hoped, Ida Lewis left her Lime Rock Lighthouse the final way she wanted—in her casket.

"Sometimes the spray dashes against these windows so thick I can't see out," she once had noted when she was 65-years-old, "and for days at a time the waves are so high that no boat would dare come near the rock, not even if we were starving. But I am happy," she had contended.

"There's a peace on this rock that you don't get on shore. There are hundreds of boats going in and out of this harbor in the summer, and it's part of my happiness to know they are depending on me to guide them safely."

The year after her death, the Annual Report of the Lighthouse Board declared her to be "the most widely known keeper in the United States." Hosea Lewis would surely have been proud of all that his daughter had accomplished. So, too, was Samuel Burgess proud that he had raised a daughter to possess a keeper's courage. No less competent than these noble daughters, however, were more than a handful of keepers' wives as well. The tale of the wife of Keeper Bray from the Cape Ann Lighthouse station on Thachers Island, just off Gloucester, is a brave one.

Aside from living at the station with their own two youngsters, the Keeper Bray and his wife were accompanied by two assistant keepers to help them maintain the twin towers in the years after the Civil War. Just before Christmas, one of the two assistants had fallen ill with a fever, and nothing they tried had seemed to help him. With a sick attendant on his hands and needing another barrel of lantern oil, the keeper decided to leave for the mainland after dawn. Aided by the healthy assistant, he took both the patient and the empty barrel, leaving behind Mrs. Bray and the children, one a toddler; the other, an infant.

Though the keepers all managed to reach mainland safely, a snowstorm arose not so long after they had left. Throughout the morning, the winds blew, the snows drifted, and visibility diminished to little, if anything at all. All this time, Mrs. Bray expected her husband to return to his station; however, by afternoon she remained alone except for the company of her youngsters. At one point, the wind tore the outside door of their dwelling clean away from its hinges. With that, the keeper's wife secured the inside door and realized her duties—the lamps would need to be trimmed and lighted.

The infant she tucked away warmly in the crib, but the toddling boy she wrapped in layers of clothing to take him to the northern tower. The distance between the two towers was the same as that between the lights at Cape Elizabeth–300 yards. But to a woman who clung to a little child, the distance was never in yards or in feet. The distance was measured in moments exposed to pelting snows and driving winds and drifts that sapped all energies. Even across so short a distance, a person—disoriented by the swirling squalls—could easily become lost, for blindness knows no shade of light. Total whiteness is no less confusing than total blackness can ever be. If Mrs. Bray had not been aware of this before she left the keeper's dwelling, then she surely learned it soon after. This was a disparaging experience.

Not surprisingly, the keeper's wife, silently hoping for some divine guidance to see her through this ordeal, was reminded of the following passage from the Bible: "But the wise took oil in their vessels with their lamps." That thought had helped maintain her courage, and both the mother and son did find the tower they had been seeking. Then, once inside, they rested.

From the base of the tower, the deck of the lantern room stood more than 160 feet above them amidst the raging winds of the snow outside. The child was too small to be left below, and yet—in this particular moment—too large to be carried up step-by-step. Still, Mrs. Bray really had no choice. She was, all at once, a mother, as well as a keeper's wife, and both were responsibilities she felt that she must keep. Together, then, the two of them began the slow and winding climb that would lead them to the still unlit lamps.

From inside the lantern room, there was nothing to see beyond the panes of glass. Nothing, that is, except snow and ice and sleet that might form on the windows. Somewhere down there stretched Thachers Island with waters that foamed at its fringes; somewhere beyond, the keeper himself was being kept from tending his light. He knew as well as his wife did, however, that the lamps would not go unattended. By early afternoon, she had trimmed the wicks and primed the light with oil. And then she set them ablaze.

A part of her duty had now been done, but that surely was not all. Another light remained to be lit, while another child needed watching. So, the keeper's wife and the keeper's son retraced their slow route to the southern tower. Inside, they repeated the dutiful routine, then returned to the keeper's dwelling alongside this southernmost tower.

Though it was already supper time, the day had been a busy one, and the night still stood ahead. The storm was winding down somewhat as she fed both her children, then put them to bed. All this time the lights were burning, and her mission could not be delayed. Soon the lamps in the northern tower would need close attention again. The same would be true of the others.

As is true with many a New England storm, the winds kept on blowing long after the snowfall had ceased. In fact, a blizzard condition has little to do with the amount of snow that will or will not cover the ground. Instead, it is always a matter of roaring winds, as well as the sight it obscures. As Keeper Bray's wife went out into the cold, she could now see the north tower's light from below. Still, the difficult path she must make toward its base had been piled high with wind-driven drifts.

In some places the gale's constant force had cleared the ground clean, but elsewhere it made up the difference. Side by side, there would be New England rocks left exposed to the darkness, then mountains of white, sculptured snow. The wind by itself would make walking a chore, but the untrodden trail to the tower was even tougher. Any snowdrift higher than the knee can prove a wearying obstacle. Lower drifts might be trudged through, but anything deeper remains unforgiving. Nevertheless, the keeper's wife did trudge and slip and push and fall and rise until she made her way up to the tower's door. Even that remained behind a drift of snow; however, once inside, she found the thickset walls provided warmth that could help to revive her.

Upstairs, she checked the wicks, then rewound the mechanism that would pump the oil for another five hours. Mrs. Bray knew that by midnight she must return, then come back again one more time before 5 a.m. Those two trips,

plus the three visits that would also be made to the lantern room in the southern tower, taxed the mother's strength. Keeping her watch on the children as well, she also kept the lights burning. Before dawn, however, she could stay awake no longer.

The next thing she knew, Mrs. Bray was awakened by the touch of her husband, who had rowed toward the lights that shined brightly through the darkness once the night's falling snow had let up. Now it was just after dawn, and the keeper's wife needed to know if their lights remained burning. "If they were not, darling," her husband is said to have answered, "I would not be here."

Together, the Bray family was safe; however, who can say how many seamen had been saved by her efforts as well? For the keeper and his family—and perhaps others unknown, too—the dawn was a time for rejoicing. It was, after all, Christmas morn.

TWO CENTURIES BESIDE THE SEA

On any given morning along this bold New England shore, the signs still appear of what has always seemed a waking, timeless life. The stars all yield their hopeful gleams to the rays of a brilliant sun; the shorebirds lift their restless wings to the rise of a stiffening breeze; and the sands and stones all cleanse themselves in the wash of a briny wave. A glorious end to a peaceful night, this kind of morning was long the dream of keepers and captains alike, but the men on the lantern galleries and the men on their quarterdecks all knew that dreams were never meant to last forever. As well, they understood that dreams were never, ever at all as they might appear; on occasion, a dream might even mask a nightmare. So much for beauty. Reality was the reason why men first built their lighthouses on this land they called New England, the nearest edge of an endless sea whose hidden dangers seemed eternal.

Even though some things never seemed to change, countless others did. By the end of the 19th century, for example, New England no longer remained a frontier, but had become instead a gateway to inland wonders. America was headed West. Some moved by prairie schooner; others, by iron horse; and more than a few, by boats that steamed along rivers and even man-made canals. This was the nation's progress, rooted deeply in earlier travels upon the ocean, where none could ever anticipate an airship. Still, New England's lighthouses remained important to its people, not only as a recognition of the shoreline's constant hazards, but also as an expression of the kinship bound together one stranger on the shore with countless others at sea. If men could not change the dangers at hand, then at least they might face them together.

After the start of the 20th century, greater changes meant fewer one for the New England shores. Less than a dozen new lighthouse stations would be

Very similar to the Graves Light at Boston Harbor, the granite shaft of Ram Island Ledge Light was completed three years later in Casco Bay off Portland, Maine.

Built in 1907, the Isle au Haut Light is the only Maine light that was built in the 20th century.

added to this coastline that held them first. Between 1900 and 1909, the government added lights at Hog Island Shoal in Rhode Island and at Graves Ledge in Boston Harbor, as well as the following in the waters off Connecticut and Maine: Greens Ledge, Peck Ledge, and New London Ledge upon Long Island Sound, then Down East at Ram Island and Isle au Haut. This slackened pace in

Built on Mark Island in 1857, the four-sided tower of Deer Island Thorofare Light was commissioned in the same year as three of the lighthouses in Vermont, but it represents only one of several tower designs then in common use. It resembles the one completed at Rhode Island's Bristol only three years earlier more than it resembles Bass Harbor Head, which was finished the following year.

the posting of the long New England shore reflected two undeniable truths: one was that these waters had become well-marked; the other was that newer ports and waterways throughout the growing nation were demanding as much attention.

Still, there were other reasons. By 1914, for example, a canal was completed to connect the waters of Cape Cod Bay with those of Buzzards Bay, just to the west of the peninsula. Basically the excavation across the Cape Cod mainland of an almost natural waterway created by the Scusset and Manomet Rivers, this canal had been envisioned as early as 1627 when Gov. Bradford first established a trading post with the Dutch along those same two brackish creeks. Later, the British had foreseen a similar advantage during the years of the Revolutionary War, and so had President Washington thereafter. When the Cape Cod Canal was finally realized in the 20th century, then, a good many prudent ship captains found reason to avoid the slower and shallower route of old that had taken their vessels through both the Vineyard and Nantucket Sounds, then around to the treacherous outer side of this angled, sandy peninsula. The canal saved time, but it also saved ships and lives.

In addition to that engineering feat, the 20th century was proving to be a period of extraordinary change. For one thing, other American ports, such as New York, had emerged, rivaled, and in many ways surpassed the older ports

With the lighthouse decommissioned and its lantern now dismantled, the classic design of Stage Harbor Lighthouse at South Chatham on Cape Cod has since become a private residence.

in New England. For another, there developed newer modes of moving both cargo and passengers. In addition, there were related improvements in ways to navigate the waters of the world.

Along with betters ways to illuminate a lighthouse lantern came progress with those invisible radio waves. After the end of World War II, radar was in widespread use. Not long after followed LORAN, which—in conjunction with the use of radar—all but eliminated the likelihood that the master of any sophisticated vessel might ever need to witness with his eyes those dangers awaiting ahead. To such seamen, the lighthouse had become little more than an ornament, a reflection of beauty and light. To the skipper of a smaller craft, however, the sight of a lighthouse still held a noble purpose. As late as the end of the first half of the century, boaters believed as much.

With the sturdy reconstruction of the original lights, along with this shrinking need for any more, the construction of lighthouses along this shoreline came to a glorious halt. The last to be commissioned in New England was the stylistic tower of Cleveland Ledge Lighthouse which sits in the waters of Buzzards Bay, not far from the western entrance to the Cape Cod Canal. Commissioned in 1943, its unique motif is not characteristic of frugal, Yankee heritage, and closely resembles instead the art deco lines of some other time and place.

While Cleveland Ledge was the last of the originals to be built in New Eng-

Almost in the shadow of the Mount Hope Bridge, the spark plug shaped tower of Hog Island Shoal Light marks the hazards between Portsmouth and Bristol, Rhode Island.

land, several others were being either decommissioned, or automated by the Coast Guard. At places such as Stage Harbor Light and Beach Point Light on Cape Cod, at Conanticut Island Light and Bristol Ferry Light in Rhode Island, and at Morgan Point Light in Connecticut, the lanterns have been removed and the dwellings have been purchased for use to this day as private homes. At

Though technically not a lighthouse, this diagram of the off-shore light tower built to replace the old Buzzards Bay Lightship of Cuttyhunk Island in the Elizabeths, is similar to the one constructed in Rhode Island waters to mark Brenton Reef.

Typical of a design more popular throughout the waters of southwestern New England, the stone dwelling with its lantern tower atop the Sheffield Island Light in Norwalk, Connecticut is identical to those stations at Block Island North in Rhode Island, at Morgan Point and Great Captain Island in Connecticut, and at New York's Old Field Point and Plum Island in Long Island Sound.

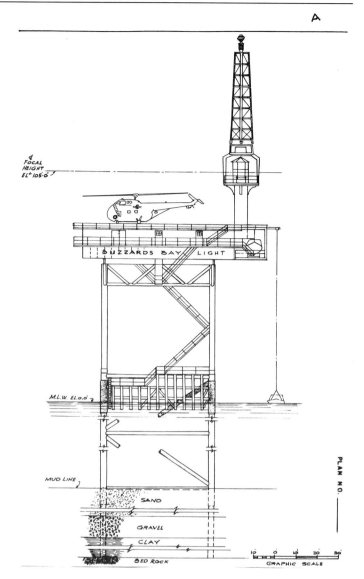

places like Monomoy Island Light south of Cape Cod, Rose Island Light in Newport, and Sheffield Island Light in Norwalk, Connecticut, the abandoned stations that once had fallen into states of unsightly disrepair have since been restored by private foundations which still recognize the heritage that rightly belongs to New England's lights.

Meanwhile, still other lighthouses have remained lighted by private owners, such as Maine's Tenants Harbor Light on Southern Island, which has become the home of artist Andrew Wyeth. On Cape Cod, the Bass River Light in West Dennis has been operated as the Lighthouse Inn for more than a half a century by the family of Robert Stone. The concern and care for restoration of abandoned lighthouses has fallen not only under the jurisdiction of several state and local historical commissions, but also within the specific concern of several private groups, such as the United States Lighthouse Society in San Francisco and the Lighthouse Preservation Society based in Rockport, Massachusetts. Some organizations hold a more limited scope, such as Friends of the Sakonnet Lighthouse in Rhode Island, while others share a concern for those lighthouses which fall within the scope of a much broader orientation, such as the Island Institute in Rockland, Maine. Regardless of their outlooks, the aim of such groups remains undeniably true, and that is to restore and preserve the lights throughout New England.

On a ledge that overlooks East Penobscot Bay, the lighthouse at Eagle Island shines out over its empty belltower, as well as the autumn foliage. As with many New England lighthouse stations that have been automated, the four-bedroom dwelling which once stood nearby has since been demolished as part of the government's policy of "site hardening."

As an altogether distinct project, however, the reconstruction of Nantucket's Great Point Light remains in a class by itself. For one thing, it is the most recently constructed lighthouse now standing on New England shores. Though the first wooden tower had been built in 1784, it was replaced with a rubblestone tower in 1816 after the original had burned to the sands the year

before. Then, in 1984, the second tower was reduced to a heap in the midst of a spring nor'easter.

Given the state of 20th century engineering and technology, any one of a number of structures could have easily been adapted and built to replace the island's northernmost lighthouse. However, the people of Nantucket wanted the new one to retain its island heritage, so the Coast Guard commissioned the Boston architectural and engineering firm of Ganteaume & McMullen to replicate the original Great Point Light. The mandate was nothing less than unique.

More than just a reproduction, the new structure took advantage of some opportunities to include engineering improvements. While the visual design is based indeed upon earlier drawings, salvaged pieces, and related historical information, its technological and structural design are based upon the most recent military specifications. The shaft of the tower is concrete coated with acrylic; the electric lighting is powered by batteries recharged with solar panels; and the cofferdam foundation is buried more than 30 feet into the beach to support a concrete mat that is fully 5 feet thick. Should Great Point itself ever wash away altogether, the lighthouse has now been designed to serve as an offshore light, not unlike the one at Cleveland Ledge. In doing this, the engineers have planned for Great Point Light to have a life cycle of 100 years.

By then, perhaps, all the other towers along New England's shores might

As at Tenants Harbor on Southern Island, Maine, the pyramid-shaped structure that serves as a companion to many lighthouse towers is the building that housed the mechanisms which sounded the fog signal.

As with almost all lighthouse lanterns, the cap above Plum Island Light in Newburyport is topped with a lightning rod. In colonial days, however, Boston Light first was not allowed to be fitted with one, because townsfolk thought it sacrilegious.

well have disappeared through lack of need and lack of any reason to retain them. Surely, no other lights will ever be built like those which once had welcomed the black New England nights and the seamen who sailed through such darkness. Yet, it is hard to imagine that this shore once stood absolutely dark.

Deep and slow and hard as rock, New England's coast has long stood tall and firm in the face on crashing breakers. Then, too, there appears the other extreme: shallow and swift and soft as sand, its land can still sweep low and weak beneath the rushing combers. Those who know New England now will say these emotions are true. And yet the sailors of the early times knew none of this at all. In this respect, at least, those mariners were no more certain than Columbus had been, and the only lights which once they had been certain of seeing were simply those which they had imagined.

As an eventual solution to their problems, though, the lighthouse has since been supplanted throughout the world. Along this crooked coast, the original stations of colonial New England were all replaced in generations past. Most of those towers and the ones built since still stand along the coast. All but Boston Light have since been automated, and a few of these stations have been abandoned by the government altogether. Given that less than a dozen New England lights were commissioned in the 20th century (none since 1943), their legions do not seem destined to grow.

The remnants of a classic structure, this rubblestone that had been used in 1818 to replace the original wooden tower of 1784 was reduced by a nor'easter in 1984 to simple rubble on the sands of Nantucket's Great Point.

Gone, then, are those lighthouses once built out of local concern. Gone just the same are the schooners and clippers, as well as the lowly shallop. And gone is the flourishing fishery that once lured the fishermen here. Gone, too, are the wicks and the wickies alike, leaving one only to imagine what those keepers who once remained awake throughout the lonely night would be thinking today if they were to learn that those ships just beyond the vast horizon no longer do peer toward their lamps, but listen instead to the wireless chatter of distant voices and a faraway code of dashes and dots. It is doubtful that those selfless souls might ever understand any way of guiding ships other than by the loom of the lighthouse, which had once been their way of life and which had once been the safest way to this part of the world, the world that began as New England.

INDEX

BIBLIOGRAPHY

ADAMS, Edward P. "Lighthouses and their Keepers." SCIENTIFIC AMERICAN, December 16, 1893. Page 387.

ADAMSON, Hans Christian. KEEPERS OF THE LIGHTS. New York: Greenberg (1955).

ALLEN, Everett S. A WIND TO SHAKE THE WORLD. Boston: Little, Brown & Company.

ANDERSON, W.P. "Lighthouse Illuminants," SCIENCE, Volume 21 (May 12, 1893).

ANONYMOUS. "The Highland Light," THE ATLANTIC MONTHLY, Volume 14, Number 86 (December, 1864).

"Lighthouses, Lightships, and Buoys," SCIENTIFIC AMERICAN, Volume 67 (September 10, 1892).

"Lighthouse Illuminants," SCIENCE, Volume 16 (November 14, 1890).

"Lighthouse Illumination," SCIENTIFIC AMERICAN, Volume 65 (June 11, 1892).

BACHAND, Robert G. NORTHEAST LIGHTS: Lighthouses and Lightships Rhode Island to Cape May, New Jersey. Norwalk, CT: Sea Sports Publications (1989).

BEARSE, Ray. MAINE: A Guide to the Vacation State. Boston: Houghton Mifflin (1969).

BIXBY, William. CONNECTICUT: A New Guide. New York: Charles Scribner's Sons (1974).

BURCHARD, John, and BUSH-BROWN, Albert. THE ARCHITECTURE OF AMERICA: A Social and Cultural History. Boston: Little, Brown & Company (1961).

CALDWELL, Bill. LIGHTHOUSES OF MAINE. Portland, ME: Gannett Books (1986).

CANDAGE, R.G.F. "Boston Light and the Little Brewsters," NEW ENGLAND MAGAZINE, Volume 13 (October, 1895).

CAPLAN, Ronald. DOWN NORTH: The Book of Cape Breton's Magazine. New York: Doubleday and Company (1980).

CARSE, Robert. KEEPERS OF THE LIGHTS: A History of American Lighthouses. New York: Charles Scribner's Sons (1969).

CHAMBERLAIN, Barbara Blau. THESE FRAGILE OUTPOSTS: A Geological Look at Cape Cod, Martha's Vineyard, and Nantucket. New York: Doubleday & Company (1964).

CLAYTON, Barbara, and WHITLEY, Kathleen. EXPLORING COASTAL NEW ENGLAND: Gloucester to Kennebunkport. New York: Dodd, Mead & Company (1979).

COLLIER, Sargent F. DOWN EAST: Maine, Prince Edward Island, Nova Scotia, and the Gaspe. New York: The Riverside Press (1953).

CONKLIN, Irving. GUIDEPOSTS OF THE SEA. New York: Macmillan Company (1939).

CONNOLLY, James B. THE BOOK OF THE GLOUCESTER FISHERMAN. New York: The John Day Company (1927).

CUSACK, Betty Bugbee. COLLECTOR'S LUCK: A Thousand Years at Lewis Bay, Cape Cod. Stoneham, MA: Barnstead Printing (1967).

DOW, George Francis, and EDMONDS, John Henry. THE PIRATES OF THE NEW ENGLAND COAST (1630-1730). New York: Argosy-Antiquarian, Ltd. (1968).

DOWNEY, Fairfax. LOUISBOURG: Key to a Continent. New York: Prentice-Hall (1965).

DRAKE, Samuel Adams. A BOOK OF NEW ENGLAND LEGENDS AND FOLK LORE. Boston: Little, Brown & Company (1901).

DRAKE, Samuel G. BIOGRAPHY AND HISTORY OF THE INDIANS OF NORTH AMERICA... Boston: The Antiquarian Institute (1837).

HAMILTON, Harlan. LIGHTS & LEGENDS: A Historical Guide to Lighthouses of Long Island Sound, Fishers Island Sound, and Block Island Sound. Stamford, CT: Westcott Cove Publishing (1987).

HAWTHORNE, Hildegarde. OLD SEAPORT TOWNS OF NEW ENGLAND. New York: Dodd, Mead & Company (1916).

HEAP, D.P. ANCIENT AND MODERN LIGHTHOUSES. Boston: Ticknor & Company (1889).

"Methods of Revolving the Optical Apparatus for Lighthouses," SCIENTIFIC AMERICAN, Volume 81 (November 25, 1899).

HEMMINGWAY, William. "The Woman of the Light," HARPERS WEEKLY, Volume 53 (August 4, 1909).

HILL, Ralph Nading. LAKE CHAMPLAIN: Key to Liberty. Woodstock, VT: The Countryman Press (1976).

HOWE, George. MOUNT HOPE: A New England Chronicle. New York: Viking Press (1959).

HOLLAND, Francis Ross Jr. AMERICA'S LIGHTHOUSES: Their Illustrated History Since 1716. Brattleboro, VT: Stephen Greene Press (1972).

HUDEN, John C. INDIAN PLACE NAMES OF NEW ENGLAND. New York: Museum of the American Indian Foundation (1962).

JOHNSON, Arnold B. THE MODERN LIGHTHOUSE SERVICE. Washington, D.C.: U.S. Government Printing Office (1890).

KITTREDGE, Henry C. CAPE COD: Its People and Their History. Boston: Houghton Mifflin Company (1968).

KOBBE, Gustav. "Heroism in the Lighthouse Service: Description of Life on Matinicus Rock, CENTURY MAGAZINE, Volume 54 (June, 1897).

    "Life in a Lighthouse," CENTURY MAGAZINE, Volume 47 (January, 1894).

    "Lighthouses and Their Keepers," SCIENTIFIC AMERICAN, Volume 69 (December 16, 1893).

LAWRENCE, C.A. "The Building of Minot's Ledge Lighthouse," NEW ENGLAND MAGAZINE, Volume 15 (October, 1896).

LUKENS, Lt. Cmdr. R.R. UNITED STATES COAST PILOT: Atlantic Coast (Section A: St. Croix to Cape Cod). Washington, D.C.: U.S. Government Printing Office (1933).

MANNING, Gordon R. LIFE IN THE COLCHESTER REEF LIGHTHOUSE. Shelburne, VT: Shelburne Museum (1958).

MILLS, Robert. THE AMERICAN PHAROS OR LIGHTHOUSE GUIDE. Washington, D.C.: Thompson & Homans (1832).

MORISON, Samuel Eliot. ADMIRAL OF THE OCEAN SEA: A Life of Christopher Columbus. Boston: Houghton Mifflin Company (1942).

    THE MARITIME HISTORY OF MASSACHUSETTS (1783-1860). Boston: Houghton Mifflin Company (1961).

MUMFORD, Lewis. STICKS & STONES: A Study of American Architecture and Civilization. New York: Dover Publications (1955).

NORDOFF, Charles. "The Lighthouses of the United States," HARPERS MAGAZINE, Volume 38 (March, 1874).

PUTNAM, George R. LIGHTHOUSES AND LIGHTSHIPS OF THE UNITED STATES. Boston: Houghton Mifflin Company (1917).

    "Beacons of the Sea," NATIONAL GEOGRAPHIC MAGAZINE, Volume 24 (January, 1913).

REDIKER, Marcus. BETWEEN THE DEVIL AND THE DEEP BLUE SEA: Merchant Seamen, Pirates, and the Aglo-American Maritime World 1700-1750. Cambridge: Cambridge University Press (1987).

ROBINSON, William F. COASTAL NEW ENGLAND: Its Life and Its Past. Boston: Little, Brown & Company (1983).

ROWE, William Hutchinson. THE MARITIME HISTORY OF MAINE: Three Centuries of Shipbuilding and Seafaring. New York: W.W. Norton & Company (1948).

SMOOK, Lt. J.M. UNITED STATES COAST PILOT: Atlantic Coast (Section B/Cape Cod to Sandy Hook). Washington, D.C.: U.S. Government Printing Office (1933).

SNOW, Edward Rowe. FAMOUS LIGHTHOUSES OF NEW ENGLAND. Boston: The Yankee Publishing Company (1945).

TAGGART, Robert. EVOLUTION OF THE VESSELS ENGAGED IN THE WATERBORNE COMMERCE OF THE UNITED STATES. Washington, D.C.:

    Navigation History NWS-83-3/U.S. Government Printing Office (1983).

THOMPSON, Sue Ellen. "The Light is My Child," THE LOG OF MYSTIC SEAPORT, Volume 32 (Fall,1980).

WHEELWRIGHT, Thea. ALONG THE MAINE COAST. American Legacy Press (1967).

WILLOUGHBY, Malcolm F. LIGHTHOUSES OF NEW ENGLAND. Boston: T.O. Metcalf Company (1929).

WITNEY, Dudley. THE LIGHTHOUSE. Boston: New York Graphic Society (1975).

ACKNOWLEDGEMENTS

Unlike a good many other arts and crafts, the fundamental act of writing is a private experience, best accomplished without some curious bystander peering at the page in progress. That is not to say, however, that a writer should be mistaken for some lonely, anti-social soul. On the contrary, every day of a writer's preparation brings some social engagement with others who roam down countless walks of life. So, though the final act of writing might well be solitary, every single writer owes an outstanding debt of gratitude to those who have provided not only the information, but also the insulation so necessary for completing the task at hand. To these folks I owe whatever I know.

At the library of the Cape Cod Community College, Charlotte Price serves not only as archivist of the Nickerson Memorial Collection, but also as an endless resource of essential information. The same is true of the indefatigable Kenneth Black, whose dedication and imagination have inspired the establishment of Maine's Lighthouse Museum at the Shore Village Museum in Rockland. To Polly Mitchell at the Shelburne Museum in Vermont, to Wick York at the Mystic Seaport in Connecticut, and to Anthony Nicolisi at the War College Museum in Newport, I am no less grateful.

In Washington, the services rendered by the historian of the United States Coast Guard, Dr. Robert Scheina, and his colleague, Robert Brownings, were unsurpassed by anyone, yet matched in their cordiality and cooperation by Ray Cotton at the Cartography Division of the National Archives. In the nation's capitol, as well, I rediscovered the legal guidance and hospitality of both Thalia Lingos and Henry Huser, to whom I owe a special thanks.

In Boston, Debra Mayer arranged to have Jay Thomas share a good part of his time reviewing with me the Great Point Lighthouse Project, which he oversaw for Ganteaume & McMullen. His explanation of blueprints, diagrams, and the entire undertaking of the island station's replication was as fascinating as it was valuable, and I appreciate their assistance.

Throughout the six state region, a good many of my counterparts extended to me their courteous cooperation in locating almost all of the photographers whose work appears in these pages. At Rhode Island Monthly, my thanks go to Managing Editor Vicki Sanders and Art Director Donna J. Chludzinski; at Vermont Life, Linda Dean Pardee; and at Maine Boats & Harbors, both Publisher John K. Hanson Jr., and Executive Editor Park Morrison. Extra special thanks in Providence are due to Sarah Gleason, whom I have only met by letter and by phone, but who has generously shared with me her extensive knowledge of the lighthouses of Rhode Island, which is the subject of her own forthcoming book. I wish her well in that endeavor. The same is true of Bill Quinn, whose published works on shipwrecks throughout Cape Cod and New England, continue to make him an invaluable swapper of facts and conversation on many days in the Nickerson Room.

To the north of New England, my gratitude is extended to Andrea Sirois of the Canadian government, and Bill Murray of the Lighthouse Monitoring Project, as well as Norman Potter of the Canadian Coast Guard, all of whom lent me assistance regarding the lighthouses of the Maritimes.

Finally, my appreciation runs deep for those who have worked with me at Quarterdeck Communications, especially when I was not there to answer a phone call or handle the correspondence. To Jodie Carter, Karen Humphries, Ellen Davies, Jamie Bazzano, and Kathy Laird, I am especially appreciative for doing all those things that they feel outside their own responsibilities. My thanks go to Rob Eckhardt and Betsy Roscoe Morin for helping me sort through countless images of lighthouse after lighthouse. And for Gale and Andy Scherding, words will never be enough. And, of course, thanks must go to my folks who took Quimby out for his walks whenever I was spending time with all these other people.

DWD
West Dennis, Cape Cod

PHOTO CREDITS